# PERSONAL BUDGET PLANNER

By
Eric P. Gelb

Personal Budget Planner
A Guide For Financial Success



Published by Career Advancement Center, Inc.



This guide contains advice about personal budgeting and finance. But the use of a book is not a substitute for legal, accounting or other professional services. Consult the appropriate professional for answers to your specific questions.

Printed in the United States of America

ISBN 0-9631289-0-6

Dedicated to:

*Max and Phil Koch,*

*the country doctor and the baker;*

*two great guys.*

## *TABLE OF CONTENTS*

This guide is designed to help you gain control over your personal finances and establish a plan to attain your financial goals:

## *TABLE OF CONTENTS (continued)*

Dear Budgeter:

This book is designed to help you gain control over your finances and gain financial freedom. You will learn how to analyze your spending habits, budget your money and build wealth. This guide should be an ongoing tool to help you plan your future and attain your financial goals. Although this is not a project to be completed in one night, it can be done in a reasonably short amount of time. And, once you digest the concepts, you should always be well ahead of the game. The first step, getting started, is the hardest, but if you procrastinate you will never win the finance game and become wealthy.

Find a clean work-space such as a desk, dining room table, or kitchen table. You will need scrap paper, your check book, bank and credit card statements, your most recent tax return, a basic electronic calculator and a pencil. To derive the most benefit from this guide, you should read the book from cover to cover and then go back and work through the examples using a pencil and the worksheets. If you prefer to manage your finances without getting into the detail of categorizing every expenditure, read the chapters and apply the concepts to your spending pattern; you will still save money.

Focus on the need to **make your money work for you**. Hopefully, you realize that money can work for or against you. The difference depends on whether you control your money. Most people lack the ability to cash their own checks or generate interest income. This means they must resort to banks who exert control over their financial destiny. Banks determine how much interest they will pay you and the monthly check charges. Everyone has been frustrated by these factors.

To further complicate matters, the interest rates banks pay fluctuate over time, and this can making servicing debts difficult. Generally, loans and credit card debts carry fixed debt rates which almost always exceed the rates banks pay on your deposits. The difference between interest income and interest expense can be relatively great, especially when market interest rates are low. For example, if your Visa card charges 21% interest on your outstanding balance and your money market account pays 5% interest, your funding shortfall equals 16% (21% minus 5%). Even when market interest rates are high your money market account may pay 11% interest while your Visa card still charges 21% interest; your interest expense still exceeds interest income by 10% (21% minus 11%). The key is to manage your money to maximize interest income over the long term.

Further, don't overlook the insurance companies who collect vast sums of money (premiums) for health, car, and homeowner's insurance. In addition, your protection by insurance may be limited as insurance companies may try to pay you less than you lost or not pay at all.

In summary, financial institutions have great control over your life, and you must control your finances to minimize your losses and maximize your wealth. Now that you have faced this unpleasant point, resolve to make every effort to work the system to your advantage. Stop the banks' and insurance companies' control over your financial well-being.

**Make your money work for you!!!**

Turn the page and conquer your finances. Good luck and enjoy. And, let me know what you think.

Eric P. Gelb
c/o Career Advancement Center, Inc.
Post Office Box 436
Woodmere, New York 11598-0436

## *WORKSHEET I - YOUR FINANCIAL GOALS:*

The best way to motivate yourself to become financially successful is to crystalize your aspirations and financial goals on paper. If you set goals and want to attain them badly enough, you should have 4 million reasons to establish a plan of action.

**What financial goals do you want to achieve?**

For some people, financial goals include paying off credit card debt, student loans, or other consumer debt. For others, their goals may include buying a condominium, house, new car or stereo, establishing a savings or retirement account; or making better use of their money. You should write your goals on paper to provide a target even though your goals can change over time as your outlook and needs change. A younger person may want to save money for college while an adult may want to buy a house or plan for retirement. Just pick a focus, and get started.

Throughout this guide, you will help a budgeter, Jack an average consumer, gain control over his finances.

Turn to Worksheet I (page 91); notice there are two examples which illustrate the concepts. The first two lines of Worksheet I contain: "Example: Buy a condominium." This worksheet is filled with lines, but it is not necessary to have many goals. Just choose one or two; or, write down many and rank them in order of importance.

1. What. Write down your goals in the column labelled "OBJECTIVE". It is helpful if your goals are realistic because when you make a financial plan, you will get closer to achieving your goals every day.

   Jack decides to buy a condominium. After reading the real estate section of the local paper, Jack notices an apartment that costs $60,000.

2. When. Jack wants to buy a condominium in four years (1995). Pick the year you want to achieve your goal and write the target year in the column marked "Year".

3. How much. It's important to assign a dollar value to your goal because you will have a tangible target to strive for. Write the dollar amount of your goal (the target amount) in the column labelled "Final Amount". Calculate this number by deciding how much money you want/need to accumulate to achieve your goal. Although Jack's dream house costs $60,000, this is not the "Final Amount" because he doesn't have to purchase the apartment with $60,000 in cash.

Jack's banker offers him a mortgage (loan) for either 80% or 90% of the cost of the condominium. [Note that the percentage down payment will vary for different properties, locations, and assets (cars, houses, etc.) and the interest rate tends to be higher when the down payment percentage is lower. Ask your banker for rate quotes and a payment schedule.]. This means Jack must make a down payment of 20% or 10% of the cost.

Jack decides to take advantage of the banker's offer and save enough money to make a 10% deposit or $6,000 ($60,000 multiplied by 10%).

Jack realizes he is not going to buy the condo until 1995, and his preferences or the price of the condo may change by then. Prices should rise if the market for housing rises, if the neighborhood becomes "hot" and everyone wants to move there, or if inflation is substantial. Jack accounts for a 20% price variance. If the condo costs $60,000 today, a reasonable estimate of the future price may be $72,000 ($60,000 plus 20% of $60,000 or 120% of $60,000). To be in a position to make a 10% down payment on a condo which costs $72,000, Jack needs to save $7,200 in four years.

Jack entered "$7,200" in the box labelled "Final Amount".

Suppose Jack, instead of wanting a condo, wanted to save money for his retirement. If his goal was to save $100,000, he would enter $100,000 in the "Final Amount" column because that is the dollar amount of his goal, the financial target. Jack might not retire for thirty years, so he would enter 2021 (1991 plus 30 years) in the column "Year".

4. The last column of Worksheet I contains the monthly deposit, the amount you have to save every month to achieve your goal. Under the two examples shown, Jack must save $136.08 or $124.08 every month (calculating the monthly deposit is covered in a later section). The specific dollar amounts are not important now, but set goals that are feasible in the desired time frame given your current financial status.

<u>For now, write down your goals</u>

in Worksheet I;

you will formulate an action plan

to achieve your goals in the subsequent chapters.

## *WORKSHEET II - YOUR NET WORTH:*

As a starting point, find out where you stand by analyzing your current financial position (your net worth).

Net worth equals: what you own minus what you owe,

and signifies the amount of earning power or buying power you have today if you use your assets (essentially your savings) to pay off what you owe (your debt).

The first section of Worksheet II (pages 92-93) is the Asset Section. Assets give you the power to build wealth by purchasing other assets such as a house or car, or by making investments. Banks use assets as collateral or security for a loan. Assets include savings accounts, money market accounts, mutual fund balances, stocks, bonds, and real estate such as a house or condominium. You can account for all your savings accounts by referring to your tax return where you presumably declared your interest income from each bank account; or, review your bank statements and passbooks.

Many people (including me) consider jewels such as diamonds to be assets, but I have excluded them from assets because my wife would be very upset if she knew I was considering hocking her diamond ring. If you own valuable jewelry, buy a rider on your homeowners insurance policy to protect your assets. Even though cars have a "Blue Book" value, I exclude them from assets because their values typically decline; generally, a car loses one-third of its value the moment you leave the dealership.

**Conduct an inventory of your assets.**

Total all your savings accounts and enter the current balance in the column marked "Total Amount". If these accounts bear interest, record the rate in the column labelled "Interest Rate". In the right-hand column marked "Monthly Payment/Income", enter the monthly amount of interest or dividend income you earn. You can calculate the monthly amount of income by dividing the estimated annual rate of return by 12 and multiplying the monthly rate by the balance. For example, if you have $1,000 in a savings account which pays 6% interest per year, your net worth should increase by approximately $5 every month ($1,000 multiplied by 6% divided by 12 months).

Next list the value of your mutual funds, your house, and any other assets you own.

After you enter all your assets, total the "Amount" column; the sum is your total assets.

If you fill out the Liability Section of Worksheet II, you may be in for a sobering experience, but it is important to get a handle on what you really owe. Liabilities are basically debts and include: credit card debts, car loans, mortgages, income taxes, and student loans. When you have recorded all your debts, total them up and enter the sum in the column labelled "Total Amount". Take a deep breath; you can pay off your debt and achieve your financial goals.

After you record all your assets and liabilities, subtract the total liabilities from your total assets. The difference is your net worth; enter your net worth in the column marked "Total Amount".

If your net worth is negative (your liabilities exceed your assets), don't worry; with Worksheet III, you can establish a plan to reduce your liabilities and increase your net worth. If your net worth is positive, set a higher goal: aim to double or triple your net worth in the next three to five years.

Remember, you can increase your net worth by increasing your assets and decreasing your liabilities. As you pay down your mortgage your liabilities decrease and your net worth should increase. Your net worth also increases if the value of your mutual funds or house increases.

## WHY IS IT GOOD TO HAVE A HIGH NET WORTH?

The person with a high net worth or sizeable personal wealth can feel secure in his future. Money in the bank enables you to buy a beautiful house for your family or a nice new car. You can feel confident in your ability to live comfortably during retirement or cover an emergency such as a medical operation.

After you determine your net worth, understand the difference between working assets and nonworking assets. **Working or liquid assets** can be converted into cash easily and include: cash, savings and money market accounts, certificates of deposit (CD's), stocks, and mutual fund balances.

**Nonworking or illiquid assets** are difficult to convert into cash. One example is your personal residence. Even though the market value of your house may rise or appreciate, the house does not generate cash which you can invest currently. So the house does not earn interest income over time. Therefore, you cannot count on the house and many other illiquid assets to generate cash to purchase other investments. On the other hand, you can utilize illiquid assets to generate cash; for example, if you rent out a room to a local college student or other boarder, the monthly rent provides income.

## Where Are You Now...What Have You Accomplished So Far?

First, you have set concrete financial goals that will help you establish a financial plan. Second, you have determined your net worth and can tie your financial position to your goals and plan a budget. Before you advance to the next section, review your financial goals in Worksheet I; you may decide to change your short term goals in light of your financial position.

## *WORKSHEET III - PERSONAL BUDGET PLANNING*

The best way to attain financial success is to gain control over your cash inflows and outflows. Worksheet III is designed to help you evaluate your spending patterns and budget your money; you will find two completed worksheets with different examples, and several blank ones you can fill in. As you work through the examples, review the sections: Tracking Daily Expenses, Credit Card Management, 82 Strategies to Save Money, and Your Checkbook to learn how to alter your spending habits to maximize your wealth.

### WHY BOTHER MAKING A BUDGET???

1. You will be able to control your money and channel more money to your discretionary spending categories.

2. You will be able to assess your financial position, change your spending patterns and attain your financial goals.

Budgeting is a simple process, but the key to successfully managing your money is self-control; everyone has a certain level of income and must make choices. The key is to manage your spending so your expenses are always less than your income. This means using self-discipline not to spend money when the expenditure hinders your financial success. The person who lives within his means should always have money and be able to build wealth.

**Set a reasonable budget**
**and stick to it,**
**and you should always have money.**

If you adhere to the following guidelines, you should be able to budget your money accurately and simply. This section requires understanding numerical examples, and if you want, take a break before you start; go to the kitchen and get a snack. While budgeting is important, it need not be a stressful task. In fact, after you budget, you should feel better since the anxiety of not really knowing your financial situation will be eliminated. Continue working on the budget when you are relaxed and can concentrate. If you have had enough for one day, put the Budget Planner away until tomorrow, but open it soon while you are still committed to the project.

Ultimately, you want a weekly budget, but first, focus on your annual budget. After all, you need to plan for lump sum items such as taxes, vacation, and holiday gifts. Each numbered paragraph in this section corresponds to a numbered line on Worksheet III. The best way to understand budgeting is to follow the explanations in the Worksheet and work through examples I (page 15) and II (page 33). Then use the blank copies in the Appendix to figure out your budget. The example assumes that only Jack is planning his budget, but if a couple is budgeting, fill in the second column labelled "Spouse or Partner". Also, keep in mind that the numbers in the example may be completely different from your experience, but use the example to understand the concepts. The theory is the same.

Note: these explanations correspond to Worksheet III, Example I (page 15).

1. **Annual gross salary** or salary before taxes. In Example I, Jack earns a "Salary before taxes" of $30,000 which appears on line number 1. Jack will receive 24 paychecks of $1,250 this year ($30,000 divided by 24). This line could be used for any sources of income such as a pension.

2. **Total withholdings:** the money your employer takes out of your pay. At a minimum, these include federal, state, and local income taxes and social security taxes. If your employer deducts health insurance premiums, add the total annual health insurance premiums you pay here. Don't forget to include your contribution to your 401K or IRA accounts, pre-tax spending accounts, withholdings for child care, and the Christmas Club. Jack earns $30,000 and his total tax rate equals 30% so he pays $9,000 ($30,000 multiplied by 30%) in taxes.

   Instead, suppose Jack pays $50 in health insurance premiums every month; his employer would deduct an additional $600 ($50 multiplied by 12 months) during the year; then his total withholdings would equal $9,600 ($9,000 in income taxes plus $600). And, if Jack contributed $1,000 to his retirement account during the year, his total deductions would equal $10,600 ($9,000 in taxes plus $600 in health insurance premiums plus $1,000 in retirement plan contributions).

   In Example I, Jack's "Total withholdings" equal $9,000.

3. **Annual net income:** subtract your Total Withholdings (line 2) from your Salary before taxes (line 1). This is the amount of money you can spend during the year without borrowing or earning extra money. Jack takes home $21,000 ($30,000 minus $9,000 in withholdings). This means Jack can spend $21,000 (in absence of other income) this year without going into debt.

4. This line begins the "**Fixed Expenses**" section and includes lines 4, 5, and 6. Fixed costs are constant every month regardless of one's lifestyle. The key to successful finance is limiting your fixed expenses because given a fixed income, the less you spend on fixed costs, the more money there is for discretionary spending and investing.

**Housing expense** is generally the largest fixed expense which could include rent or mortgage payments. Don't forget the additional monthly condominium maintenance (common area charges) and property tax payments. Suppose you own a condo and your monthly mortgage payment equals $408 and your monthly maintenance equals $150. Your total monthly housing cost equals $558, and your annual housing cost would equal $6,696 ($558 multiplied by 12 months).

Jack rents an apartment and the monthly rent equals $508, so he entered $6,096 on line 4.

5. **Loans.** Line 5 is a painful remainder of how much money you have to pay to service your loans. Under the category Loans, include credit card debt, car loans, student loans, home equity loans and personal loans, but the list is not necessarily all-inclusive (review the chapter Borrowing Money). Let's assume Jack owns his car free and clear of any loans, but has a student loan and the monthly payment equals $115. Every year, he must pay $1,380 ($115 multiplied by 12 months). Jack entered $1,380 on line 5.

6. **Insurance premiums** should be entered on line 6. If your employer does not provide health insurance and you have your own policy, enter your annual cost here. Also, include your other insurance costs: car, home, and life. Every year, Jack pays home owner's and auto insurance premiums equal to $135 and $900, respectively and entered $1,035 on line 6. Never skimp on expenditures such as health insurance, home-owner's insurance or renter's insurance. Also, it may be worthwhile to buy disability insurance in case you become unable to work. If you are married or have children, you should consider buying term life insurance. Regarding health insurance, younger people can sometimes save money by joining their parents' health insurance plan. Also, health maintenance organizations ("HMO's") can provide a cost savings.

7. **Total fixed living expenses.** Line 7: the sum of lines 4, 5, and 6. These are fixed expenses because every month, you must pay the same amount regardless of your income or spending habits. While it is true that if you rent a house or apartment, you might decide to cancel your lease or move to another apartment when your lease ends, but in the short run, these costs are fixed. You can reduce your rent by sharing an apartment. Jack's "Total fixed expenses" equal $8,511.

8. This section is the "**Periodic Costs**", expenses which are unavoidable but can be managed. The first one is your **Commuting cost.** This could be the cost of a bus ticket, railroad pass, or gasoline, parking and tolls for your car. Figure out your monthly cost and multiply the monthly number by 12. Jack's monthly commuting cost equals $55; therefore, his annual cost equals $660 ($55 multiplied by 12 months). $660 appears on line 8. This category can include the cost of your pet (food, veterinarian, grooming, and boarding); or tuition for school or any other recurring expenditure.

9. **Personal beauty care**: haircuts, nail salon, health club, dry cleaner, etc. These costs are important to make you look and feel good. Consider choosing a different hair salon or visiting your hairdresser every 5 weeks instead of every 4 because you will save money. Consider buying clothes you can wash instead of those which require dry cleaning. If Jack gets his hair cut once a month and loves the tanning salon he may spend $50 every month or $600 annually.

10. **Medical costs not covered by insurance** (line 10). It is smart to opt for the best care regardless of the cost, and assume you will incur these costs and cannot change their nature or amount. Jack spends approximately $500 on visits to doctors, contact lenses, eyeglasses, medicine, trips to the pharmacy, and the deductible on his health insurance plan.

11. **Car repair and maintenance costs** (line 11). These vary with the age of your car and driving habits. Of course, if you don't own a car, your maintenance costs should equal zero. Jack expects to spend $1,200 this year to keep his car running. See 82 Strategies to Save Money to reduce your car maintenance costs.

12. **Income tax.** Some people don't pay enough income tax during the year and must make quarterly estimated payments to Uncle Sam. Your employer withholds income taxes based on your annual salary, but if you earn income from a second job or interest and dividend income and do not have additional income taxes withheld, you may owe more tax.

    Jack's salary is $30,000, and his employer withholds $9,000 in taxes. If Jack earns money from a second job or in the form of interest and dividends, Jack will earn more than $30,000 in income; therefore, he will owe income tax on the additional income. In this example, Jack will have to make four quarterly payments of $100: one in January, March, June, and September. Jack has entered $400 on line 12.

13. **Total periodic costs**: add up lines: 8, 9, 10, 11, and 12. Jack's costs equal $3,360.

14. This section is the "**Ongoing Out of Pocket Expenses**", expenses which can be managed with a little motivation and some discipline. One way Jack can look at how much money is available for discretionary spending is to compare his income with his total fixed and periodic costs; he can spend what's left without running a deficit.

    **Cash spending budget**. Jack is generous with himself and withdraws $150 from the bank every week. Jack is like most of us; he takes out a lot of cash every week, and the money seems to disappear quickly, much to his dismay. This equates to $7,800 every year ($150 multiplied by 52 weeks). To determine how much you spend every week, check your bank statements and total your withdrawals, review the section: Tracking Daily Expenses.

15. **Credit card payments.** To boot, Jack loves to use his six Visa and Mastercards. He typically spends $400 every month or $4,800 every year. Jack spends a large percentage of this amount on dining out, clothing, and entertainment. Review the section: Credit Card Management.

16. **Gifts.** Jack spends approximately $300 on gifts annually. Typically, he and his friends exchange birthday gifts; this year, they have decided not to give gifts.

17. **Telephone/utilities.** Since Jack is very popular, he calls many friends on the telephone. His monthly telephone and utility bills total $50 or $600 every year ($50 multiplied by 12).

18. **Other.** No worksheet would be complete without an "Other" line because inevitably, someone has a spending habit which does not fit any of the categories on lines 1 - 17. Several items to include on Line 18 are donations to charities, church or temple dues, home furnishings, and club memberships. In fact, this category can be quite expensive, and should be reviewed carefully, because a lot of money can disappear into the "Other" category. Jack has spent so much money which he entered in the previous lines on Worksheet III, he has no "Other expenses".

19. **Total out of pocket**: add up lines 14, 15, 16, 17, and 18. Remember the amount of out-of-pocket money you spend because this is the easiest category to manage. Jack's total out of pocket expenses equal $13,500.

20. **Other income.** Perhaps (a) your relatives gave you money which you were smart enough to save, (b) you have built wealth and earn income every year, (c) you have stocks or CDs which pay dividends or interest, (d) you earn overtime pay, have a second job, or earn a bonus, or (e) some other item. This line appears near the bottom of the worksheet to stress that you should not count on your "Other income" for spending money. Rather, you should use your "Other income" to build wealth. Jack earns "other income" of $500 - interest income from his savings accounts.

21. **Net Surplus** or **(Deficit).** This is the amount of money you have left before taking into account your vacation allowance and annual savings goal. Figure out this amount by using this formula: Line 3 minus Line 7 minus Line 13 minus Line 19 plus Line 20. If this number is negative (less than zero), reconsider your spending habits. Jack has overdone it a little this year; his deficit is $3,871.

22. **Vacation** is one of the last lines of this worksheet because it should be the last item you consider when planning your finances. Picture yourself sitting on a warm beach in the Caribbean sipping a cool pina colada. The waves come up to your lounge chair and you dip your feet in. This is beautiful. Jack likes trips like this and intends to spend $3,000 on vacations this year. But, can he afford this trip? If yes, he should go for it. If not, maybe he should take a trip like this every other year or every third year. For the first draft of your budget, pick a number and enter it on line 22; you can adjust your plans later.

23. **Annual savings goal**. Jack has decided to save $136.08 every month or $1,633 this year. Although this line is the last one on the page, it is the most important. The vacation allowance and the savings goal probably mean the difference between a deficit or surplus. Regardless of your financial position, budget some money for savings. Set aside money to establish an emergency fund (the fund could save you during a medical illness or in the event you lose your job). Even if you owe Visa $25,000, save $25, $50, or even $100 every month and pay off your credit card balances at the same time. When you finish paying off your credit card debt, you will have built wealth.

24. **Total surplus or deficit** (line 21 minus line 22 minus line 23). Be sure your assumptions are correct. If you have a deficit as Jack does, read on. Based on Jack's projected budget, he will spend $8,504 more than he will earn this year. And, unfortunately, deficits tend to snowball.

    Now, you have analyzed Jack's preliminary budget. Read the next sections to see how to manage your expenses and how Jack can cut his deficit. When you are ready, use the blank copies of Worksheet III (pages 94 - 96) to plan your own budget.

# WORKSHEET III

## PERSONAL BUDGET PLANNER (EXAMPLE I)

| | | Yourself | Partner | Total |
|---|---|---|---|---|
| | INCOME: | | | |
| 1 | Salary before taxes: | $30,000 | | $30,000 |
| 2 | Total withholdings: | 9,000 | | 9,000 |
| 3 | Net income: | $21,000 | | $21,000 |
| | FIXED EXPENSES: | | | |
| 4 | Housing expenses: | 6,096 | | 6,096 |
| 5 | Loan payments: | 1,380 | | 1,380 |
| 6 | Insurance premiums: | 1,035 | | 1,035 |
| 7 | Total fixed expenses: | $8,511 | | $8,511 |
| | PERIODIC COSTS: | | | |
| 8 | Commuting cost: | 660 | | 660 |
| 9 | Personal beauty care: | 600 | | 600 |
| 10 | Medical costs: | 500 | | 500 |
| 11 | Car repair costs: | 1,200 | | 1,200 |
| 12 | Income tax payments: | 400 | | 400 |
| 13 | Total periodic costs: | $3,360 | | $3,360 |
| | ONGOING OUT OF POCKET EXPENSES: | | | |
| 14 | Cash spending budget: | 7,800 | | 7,800 |
| 15 | Credit card payments: | 4,800 | | 4,800 |
| 16 | Xmas, birthday, gifts: | 300 | | 300 |
| 17 | Telephone / utilities: | 600 | | 600 |
| 18 | Other expenses: | 0 | | 0 |
| 19 | Total out of pocket: | $13,500 | | $13,500 |
| 20 | Other income: | 500 | | 500 |
| 21 | Net surplus (deficit): | ($3,871) | | ($3,871) |
| 22 | Vacation allowance: | 3,000 | | 3,000 |
| 23 | Savings goal: | 1,633 | | 1,633 |
| 24 | Total surplus (deficit): | ($8,504) | | ($8,504) |

## *TRACKING DAILY EXPENSES*

Many people withdraw money from the bank whenever their wallet is bare. This practice leads to confusion and lack of financial control. Suppose you set out to spend $100 every week, and on Monday morning, you visit the bank and withdraw $100 from your checking account. But, by Friday, you realize that you spent the entire $100 and take out another $100 which you spend during the weekend. This week, you spent $200, double your budget. This is one way to run a deficit.

Many people face this dilemma, and it is relatively easy to correct:

1. Experiment with different Cash Spending Budgets until you find one that works for you, but **never expand your budget to meet your spending habits.** There are two ways to set a weekly cash budget: 1) Work through Worksheet III to determine how much money you can afford to spend without running a deficit; or 2) Calculate the minimum amount of money you need to spend every week (food and commuting) and add an allowance for entertainment and extras.

2. Spend less than your budget. If you can afford to spend $120 every week, budget $100; you should save $80 every month ($120 minus $100 or $20 multiplied by 4).

3. Don't think that because you have a positive balance in your checking account, you are free to withdraw money as you please. Establish a specific day when you will withdraw your weekly Cash Spending Budget from your checking account. Generally, Sunday night or Monday morning is ideal. And, withdraw your entire weekly balance at once.

4. Don't spend more than your budget. Limit your expenditures to your budget and don't return to the bank until next week. Once you establish a Cash Spending Budget (line 14 of Worksheet III) that is reasonable for you, stick to it. Discipline yourself to spend your weekly cash budget amount or less; then you should always have money.

Some people have no idea how much cash they spend every week. It's easy to figure out how much cash you spend by reviewing your bank statements or your checkbook. Write down your withdrawals for the last three to six months and see how much money you withdraw from the bank every month. Multiply the amount of cash you withdrew from the bank during the last six months by two; this is approximately the amount of cash you spend during the last year. Enter this amount on line 14 of Worksheet III.

Most people I talk with have the same difficulty:

**they have no idea where they spend their cash.**

The answer: buy a pocket-sized notebook from a stationery store and carry it with you everywhere you go. Make an entry in your notebook for every item you spend money on. Suppose you withdraw $100 from the bank every Monday; keep track of every penny you spend. If you do this for several months, you should develop an understanding of how you spend your money. Once you know where you spend your money, you can better manage your money.

<u>Here is a List of Common Spending Areas:</u>

Books
Breakfast
Candy/snacks
Commuting
Dinner
Drinks after work
Dry cleaner/laundry
Entertainment (movies)
Groceries
Lunch
Newspapers/magazines
Personal beauty care (haircuts, manicure)
Pharmacy
Stamps
Supplies (pens, paper, envelopes)
Transportation (parking, taxis, gasoline)

Review your expenditures and consider reducing the unnecessary ones. By reducing your spending in some categories, you should have more money for vacations, entertainment, or wealth-building.

## *CREDIT CARD MANAGEMENT*

It is very easy to use credit cards because almost every store and restaurant accepts them. And, it seems that the bill will come due some time in the future and somehow you will have the money to pay the bill. The key is to know how much you can charge on your credit cards and still pay off the entire balance (figure this out by reviewing Worksheet III), and don't charge more than you can afford to pay off in full. It is best to pay the entire bill when it is due because the credit card companies typically charge 20% interest on the outstanding balance, a hefty rate at any time. At interest rates of 20%, if you don't make any payments, the amount of money you owe will double every 3.6 years. And, as your credit card company charges interest on your balance due the sooner you reduce the balance, the lower your interest expense will be.

Five myths about credit cards:

Myth 1: Credit card companies make it extremely easy for cardholders to pay a fraction of the balance due because it is good for the consumer.

Myth 2: Since the credit card is not cash, people don't actually have to pay their charges.

Myth 3: The charges will come due sometime in the future and there is no reason to worry about paying the bill.

Myth 4: Borrowing from credit cards will solve financial problems.

Myth 5: Borrowing from one credit card to pay off another credit card bill is a good idea.

CREDIT CARD TROUBLE IS A SERIOUS SITUATION
WHICH CALLS FOR DRASTIC ACTION TO FIX IT.

DON'T SPEND MORE MONEY ON YOUR CREDIT CARDS
THAN YOU CAN PAY IN FULL.

IF YOU DON'T HAVE A STEADY SOURCE OF INCOME,
DON'T USE YOUR CREDIT CARDS.

THE SOLUTION TO CREDIT CARD TROUBLE:
LOCK THEM IN YOUR DRAWER OR CANCEL THEM!!!

IF YOU CANNOT CONTROL YOURSELF WITH YOUR CREDIT CARDS,
DON'T CARRY THEM IN YOUR WALLET!!!

It is easy to spend money on credit cards, so it pays to analyze your monthly statements periodically, especially if you carry large balances. Here are items that appear regularly on my statements:

Automobile repairs
Books
Charitable donations
Clothing
Compact Discs/cassette tapes
Electronics (stereos)
Entertainment (concerts, theater)
Flowers
Gasoline
Gifts
Groceries
Household items/home furnishings
Household repairs
Pharmacy
Restaurant charges
Vacation bills (airfare, hotels)

If you have accumulated a huge balance on your credit cards, here are a few remedies to pay off the debt:

1. Stop using your credit cards until you pay off the debt; cut them in half if necessary.

2. Instead of spending more money on your credit cards, use the amount you budgeted for credit card spending to pay off the outstanding debt. In addition, pay as much money as possible to reduce your credit card debt.

3. Consider borrowing from one credit card which charges a lower interest rate to pay off your debt on a higher-interest rate card. Use the money from the second credit card to pay off your debt on the first card. The key is not to double the amount of debt you started with.

4. As a last resort, get a debt consolidation loan (only upon advice of an accountant or financial advisor). If you do get such a loan, use the proceeds to pay off your credit card debt, establish a monthly mandatory payment schedule, and don't incur more credit card debt.

It is a good idea to save your credit card receipts until the bill arrives; then compare the statement with the receipts to ensure the charges are correct. After you check to see that the charges match the receipts, discard all the receipts except those from purchases which are tax deductible. Also, consider saving the monthly credit card statements for about one year for reference; if you charge tax deductible expenses, you should keep your credit card statements on file for about 7 years. If you have already tossed your monthly statements into the trash, your bank should send you copies.

Once you know where you spend your money, make choices and trim your expenditures. Also, study the credit card section of: 82 Strategies to Save Money. Suppose your November Visa bill shows you ate dinner in restaurants 14 times. This means you went out for dinner almost every other night. Instead, go out once or twice a week and invite people to your house. Review your spending habits and reduce the frequency of your credit card usage.

## *YOUR CHECKBOOK*

Many of us write checks blindly every month. Sometimes, there is money to cover the checks, and unfortunately, sometimes the checks bounce.

You can figure out how much money you spend in each category by reviewing your checkbook. Review your checkbook for the last year and use scrap paper to divide your expenses into categories. List each check by category to determine how much you spend in each area. Make a mental note of how you spend your money.

Here is a list of expenditures or organizations consumers typically pay by check:

Automobile repair shops
Book and record clubs
Charities
Commuter railroad (monthly ticket)
Condominium maintenance (common area charges)
Credit card companies
Department stores (for house credit cards)
Doctors
Dry cleaners/laundry
Government (income taxes)
Grocery stores/supermarket
Hair salons
Insurance companies
Loan companies (student loans, car loans, mortgage)
Long distance telephone companies
Mail order products
Municipalities (parking tickets)
Oil companies (gasoline purchases)
Pharmacy
Relatives for gifts
Rent (landlord)
Subscriptions (newspapers, magazines)
Utilities (electricity, telephone)

Once you understand where you spend your money, delve into the categories and trim or eliminate some expenses.

Keep good records, and you will better control your money. Record all transactions, and reconcile your checkbook every month.

## *BORROWING MONEY (YOUR LOANS)*

Most Americans are in debt in one way or another, either through mortgage debt associated with buying a house or condominium, student loans, or credit cards. It is easy to borrow money, but few people consider the effects of taking out a loan.

1. The borrower must make monthly payments throughout the entire term (life) of the loan which means the borrower will have less discretionary money to spend.

   If you filled in Worksheet III, you can estimate how much money you have left over after paying your fixed and periodic expenses. But, consider that most people spend all their income, and maybe even more than their income. So, taking out a loan entails making a sacrifice. Therefore, it is important to calculate how much you can reduce your spending money to service a loan and still live the lifestyle you are accustomed to. Only you can determine how much money you can safely borrow and still meet your monthly payment obligations.

   Jack's salary after taxes equals $21,000, (based on Worksheet III, example I), his other income equals $500, and he spends $8,511 on fixed expenses and $3,360 on periodic costs. This means Jack has $9,629 ($21,000 plus $500 minus $8,511 minus $3,360) left to spend before facing a deficit. Of course, Jack must eat, and he wants to enjoy himself, so he will probably spend most of the $9,629, leaving little for monthly loan payments.

   Suppose Jack wants to borrow $5,000 (the principal) to buy a new car. Jack's banker might offer a loan which must be paid off in 5 years (60 months) at 10%, and Jack would be required to make monthly loan payments of $106. Every year, Jack would pay $1,272 ($106 monthly payment multiplied by 12 months per year). In absence of any additional income, now Jack can spend only $8,357 ($9,629 minus $1,272 in loan payments) on discretionary items. Maybe Jack's current income level and spending habits will allow him to service this loan; or, he can reduce his other expenditures to make the loan payments, or he can borrow less money or keep his old car.

   Jack should be aware that if he fails to meet the loan payments, the bank may repossess his car. Then he will have to return to public transportation.

   Monthly loan payments will include the interest on the loan plus amortization (retirement) of principal. Jack eyes a new sports car and hopes to buy it by borrowing $10,000 from a bank that is charging 7% interest. As a rule of thumb, the interest charges for the first year will be approximately $700 ($10,000 loan balance multiplied by 7% interest rate), and the monthly interest charge should be $58.33 ($700 annual interest divided by 12 months per year).

Don't overlook the principal payments. You can calculate the approximate monthly principal payment by dividing the loan balance by the total number of monthly payments. Jack's banker requires him to repay the loan in 5 years or 60 months (5 years multiplied by 12 months per year). Therefore, Jack must pay approximately $166.67 ($10,000 desired loan divided by 60 months to repay loan) in principal every month.

Therefore, Jack's approximate monthly payment including principal and interest should equal $225 ($58.33 in interest plus $166.67 in principal). Every year Jack must budget $2,700 ($225 monthly loan payment multiplied by 12 months per year) to service the $10,000 loan. Given Jack's income level and spending habits, he should consider keeping his old car.

2. Monthly loan payments are based on the size of the loan, the term of the loan, and the interest rate.

    a) Outstanding balance. The outstanding balance is the remaining amount to be paid on the loan after each monthly payment. Interest is charged on the outstanding loan balance so the higher the loan balance, the more interest Jack will pay. Also, the more money Jack borrows, the more money he will have to repay.

    b) Term of the loan. The term of the loan is the number of months or years in which you are required to repay the loan; short term loans may have terms of one year or less, and mortgages may have a term as long as 30 years. The longer the term of the loan, the longer the loan balance will be outstanding. And, the higher the outstanding balance, the more interest Jack will pay. If Jack pays off his $5,000 loan at 10% over 60 months, he might pay $106 every month or $6,360 ($106 multiplied by 60 months) in total. If Jack pays off the loan over 10 years or 120 months, he might pay approximately $66 every month or $7,920 ($66 multiplied by 120 months) in total. The $1,560 ($7,920 minus $,6,360) difference arises because Jack pays off the 5 year loan quicker than the ten year loan, and the bank charges less interest on the 5-year loan.

    c) Interest rate charged. The interest rate charged is the percent of the loan that the bank will charge for the use of its money. The higher the interest rate, the greater the borrower's cost. Obviously, a loan with a 10% interest rate costs more than a loan with an 8% interest rate. For example, if Jack borrows $10,000 at 10% interest, he might pay $1,000 in interest during the first year of the loan. But, if the same loan bears an 8% interest rate, the interest in the first year might be only $800. Given the same life of the loan, the higher the interest rate, the higher the monthly payment.

The interest rate on a loan may be fixed (the same rate is charged over the entire life of the loan) or floating (the interest rate changes every quarter or six months based on an index. One commonly used index is treasury bonds - the interest rate on your loan might be 2% over the 10-year treasury bond rate so when the treasury bond rate changes, your mortgage rate may change).

**Paying Loans**

When people borrow money, the bank provides a monthly payment schedule or a monthly payment coupon book. Monthly loan payments are based on the size of the loan, the term of the loan, and the interest rate. Consider loan theory:

a) Banks charge interest on the outstanding loan balance.

b) Monthly payments are applied first to the interest charge.

c) Any money in excess of the interest charge reduces the principal.

d) Therefore, the lower the outstanding loan balance, the lower the interest paid.

After determining the amount of money to be borrowed, and negotiating and shopping around for the lowest interest rate, consider these strategies Jack should implement to reduce the amount of money he will pay to retire the loan:

Example:

The following assumptions reflect the terms of Jack's loan contract and are reflected in line 1 of the table below:

| | |
|---|---:|
| Loan amount: | $100,000 |
| Contractual term of loan: | 30 years |
| Number of months: | 360 months |
| Annual interest rate: | 12% |
| Monthly interest rate: | 1% |
| Required monthly loan payment: | $1,029 |
| Total payments per loan contract: | $370,300 |

see table on next page...

Loan Table

| | Extra Monthly Payment | Actual Monthly Payment | Actual Total Payments | Life of Loan | Savings Over Contractual Loan |
|---|---|---|---|---|---|
| 1 | $0 | $1,029 | $370,300 | 30 years | --- |
| 2 | $25 | $1,054 | $315,354 | 25 years | $54,946 |
| 3 | $50 | $1,079 | $283,889 | 22 years | $86,411 |
| 4 | $171 | $1,200 | $216,031 | 15 years | $154,269 |
| 5 | --- | $1,000 | $460,000 | 30 years | ($89,700) |
| 6 | --- | $500 | $2,027,482 | 30 years | (1,657,180) |

The following explanations correspond to the numbered lines in the above table:

1. Required monthly loan payment; Jack merely repays the loan in accordance with the loan agreement. Jack pays $1,029 every month and retires the loan in 30 years. His total payments are $370,300 ($1,029 multiplied by 360 months).

2. Required monthly loan payment plus $25 every month. Jack pays the required $1,029 plus $25 every month for a total monthly payment of $1,054. Before increasing the monthly loan payments, Jack should consider the effect the additional payments will have on his budget. This is important because regardless of the size of Jack's payment in any one month, the bank still requires him to make the minimum payment of $1,029 every month.

   In this case, Jack repays the loan in 25 years, and his total loan payments equal $315,354. He saves $54,946 compared with the contractual loan. Notice how powerful a small additional payment is. The savings occur because the additional payments reduce the outstanding loan balance and therefore lower the interest charges.

3. Required monthly loan payment plus $50 every month. Jack pays the required $1,029 plus $50 every month for a total monthly payment of $1,079. In this case Jack repays the loan in 22 years, and his total loan payments equal only $283,889. Jack saves $86,411.

4. In this case, Jack decides to repay his loan in only 15 years, half the contractual life of 30 years. By paying an additional $171 every month, Jack can retire the loan in 15 years, and he should save $154,269. Notice that Jack does not have to double his monthly payment in order to pay off his loan in half the time.

5. Interest-only. In this case, Jack's monthly payment equals the interest on the outstanding balance: in this case $1,000 ($100,000 loan balance multiplied by the monthly interest rate of 1%). Since Jack pays only the monthly interest charge, the loan balance stays constant over the term of the loan (it is highly unlikely that anyone would extend an interest-only loan for 30 years). Jack pays only the $1,000 interest bill every month, and at the end of the 30th year, he must repay the $100,000. Jack's total payments equal $460,000 ($1,000 monthly interest charge multiplied by 360 months plus the $100,000 loan balance). For the privilege of paying interest only, Jack loses $89,700 compared with the contractual loan.

6. Negative amortization. This case is also highly unlikely because Jack would be in default on his loan, but this concept is relevant to credit card debt. Suppose Jack pays only $500 every month, approximately half the required $1,029 payment. Remember, the bank charges interest on Jack's outstanding loan balance. In this case, the loan balance increases because Jack's payment is less than the monthly interest charge. If Jack pays only $500 every month, at the end of the 30th year, the loan balance should grow to $1,847,482, an astronomical sum. Assuming Jack didn't lose his house and could afford to pay the final outstanding loan balance, Jack would pay $2,027,482 in total. The cost of this repayment plan is $1,657,180 compared with the contractual loan. Keep that in mind every time you use your credit cards and don't pay off the full balance.

In summary, implement these strategies to cut your total loan payments:

1. Increase your monthly payments as illustrated on lines 2 and 3 of the table.

2. Periodically, make an extra payment to reduce the outstanding loan balance. Suppose Jack borrows $10,000 at 10% interest; Jack might pay $1,000 ($10,000 outstanding balance multiplied by 10% interest rate) in interest during the first year. Suppose Jack borrows the $10,000 at 10%, but the next day, Jack's parents reduce his loan balance by $500. Now, the outstanding loan balance is only $9,500, and the interest for the first year might be only $950 ($9,500 outstanding balance multiplied by 10% interest rate). Due to the lower outstanding loan balance Jack will pay less interest over the life of the loan.

3. Shorten the term of the loan (possibly in half as illustrated on line 4).

Other Points:

1. Be sure the loan contract states there will be no penalties for prepayments.

2. Borrowers are obligated to make the contractual loan payment every month so don't make extra payments if you may be unable to make the contractual payment next month.

3. Beware of extra up-front or supplemental interest charges because they increase the cost of your loan. One example is "points" which is an up-front charge which can be as high as 3% of the loan balance. Suppose Jack borrows $100,000 and pays 3 points or $3,000. In effect, Jack borrows only $97,000 ($100,000 minus $3,000); yet he still pays the contractual interest rate based on a borrowing of $100,000. Points raise the effective cost of borrowing.

If you are eager to reduce the overall cost of your loans, implement one of the above strategies. You will be surprised how much money you will save.

## *MAKING FINANCIAL CHOICES - WORKSHEET III (Jack's Example II):*

See page 33.

The first point to consider when establishing a financial plan is: You pay for everything you do. Spend now, and you may have no money later. If you save now and your money grows, you will have less spending money today and more wealth tomorrow.

In order to control your money, you must think of money as a good ("product") just like eggs or steak. It's obvious that one can obtain more money by borrowing or earning more money (higher salary, over-time, or second job) and end up with less by spending too much or using credit card debt. Remember, if you borrow money, you must repay the loan plus interest. You can make your money work for you by establishing financial policies to stretch your money. Review the sections: 82 Strategies to Save Money and Wealth - Building Strategies.

My High School Social Studies Class discussed investing in guns or butter where a country could choose to buy guns and ammunition to defend the country which would eventually lead to a stronger country and the power to build wealth. On the other hand, butter is a one-time consumable product which disappears once you eat it. Building wealth is analogous to this concept. If a person earns a fixed salary and spends all of it on entertainment, food, and clothing, there will be no money left to build wealth. If, on the other hand, a person doesn't spend any money on butter and invests all his money in guns (assuming guns will provide a return on investment), he should amass great wealth (and possibly starve in the process). It is important to realize that it takes money to earn money (build wealth). To amass wealth, one must set aside money for savings and investment, but also strike a balance between investing (guns) and spending (butter).

Jack reconsidered his high style of living (at least on paper) and prepared a second budget. Compare Worksheet III, Examples I and II to see where Jack plans to cut his expenditures. Jack still has his job which pays $30,000 and his take-home pay equals $21,000. Jack is unable to change his fixed costs, but he could change his Periodic Costs.

Jack needs to take the bus to work, so his commuting costs are fixed at $660. In addition, his medical costs, car repair costs, and income tax payments are fixed. He reconsidered his tanning salon and other beauty care budget (line 9) which totalled $600. By sitting in his backyard and getting a haircut less frequently, Jack decides to spend only $300 on beauty care. This means a $300 saving.

Jack's biggest cash leakage is his Cash Spending Budget which is currently $150 per week or $7,800 per year (line 14). Jack decides to reign in his spending; he will strive to spend only $75 per week or $3,900 this year. If Jack spends only $3,900, he should save $3,900. A reduction from $150 to $75 is a drastic cut and may not be feasible in light of the expenditures Jack must make. Jack could aim for $75 and spend $100 per week; this still represents a significant savings.

Jack buys new clothes every month, but upon looking in his closet, he sees he can create new outfits by mixing and matching clothes he already owns. In addition, he decides to eat at less expensive restaurants and eat home more often. His aim is to cut his credit card expenses (line 15) from $4,800 this year to $2,000. $2,000 per year equates to $167 per month. If Jack spends only $2,000 on his credit cards this year, he should save $2,800. This may be a drastic cut, but Jack's heart and mind are moving in the right direction. Jack can strive to spend $2,000 on credit cards this year, actually spend $3,000 and still save $1,800 from his original plan.

Jack decides to reduce his expenditures on gifts (line 16) from $300 to $200.

Jack reviews his utility expenses (line 17) and realizes he runs the heater and the air conditioner simultaneously; in addition he leaves all the lights on, even when he leaves his apartment. He also decides to call his friends less frequently and during discount calling periods. He estimates he can save $350 ($600 minus $250) in this category.

Jack is really intent on buying his condominium in 1995, so he decides to get a second job. He estimates he can earn $2,589 (after-tax; see Worksheet VIII) by working every Saturday. Jack's original entry on line 20 goes from $500 to $3,089 ($2,589 plus $500).

Jack remembers his last vacation to the Caribbean and longs to return, but decides to savor the memories with his photos. He plans to take less expensive vacations or fewer trips this year which cost $1,500 instead of $3,000. This should yield a $1,500 saving.

Jack revises his savings goal and decides to save $124.08 every month in order to accumulate the down payment for the condo. His aim is to save $1,489 this year.

All in all, Jack turned an $8,504 deficit into a $90 surplus. He could save this money for his down payment or he might reduce any credit card debt.

It is certainly much easier to create a surplus on paper than it is to create one in reality, but with motivation and discipline, you can gain control over your finances and create a surplus every year. You will clear up your debts faster than you think and build wealth.

**MAKE A PLAN,**

**PUT IT INTO ACTION,**

**AND STICK TO IT!!!**

# WORKSHEET III

## PERSONAL BUDGET PLANNER (EXAMPLE II)

| | | Yourself | Partner | Total |
|---|---|---|---|---|
| | INCOME: | | | |
| 1 | Salary before taxes: | $30,000 | | $30,000 |
| 2 | Total withholdings: | 9,000 | | 9,000 |
| 3 | Net income: | $21,000 | | $21,000 |
| | FIXED EXPENSES: | | | |
| 4 | Housing expenses: | 6,096 | | 6,096 |
| 5 | Loan payments: | 1,380 | | 1,380 |
| 6 | Insurance premiums: | 1,035 | | 1,035 |
| 7 | Total fixed expenses: | $8,511 | | $8,511 |
| | PERIODIC COSTS: | | | |
| 8 | Commuting cost: | 660 | | 660 |
| 9 | Personal beauty care: | 300 | | 300 |
| 10 | Medical costs: | 500 | | 500 |
| 11 | Car repair costs: | 1,200 | | 1,200 |
| 12 | Income tax payments: | 400 | | 400 |
| 13 | Total periodic costs: | $3,060 | | $3,060 |
| | ONGOING OUT OF POCKET EXPENSES: | | | |
| 14 | Cash spending budget: | 3,900 | | 3,900 |
| 15 | Credit card payments: | 2,000 | | 2,000 |
| 16 | Xmas, birthday, gifts: | 200 | | 200 |
| 17 | Telephone / utilities: | 250 | | 250 |
| 18 | Other expenses: | 0 | | 0 |
| 19 | Total out of pocket: | $6,350 | | $6,350 |
| 20 | Other income: | 3,089 | | 3,089 |
| 21 | Net surplus (deficit): | $3,079 | | $3,079 |
| 22 | Vacation allowance: | 1,500 | | 1,500 |
| 23 | Savings goal: | 1,489 | | 1,489 |
| 24 | Total surplus (deficit): | $90 | | $90 |

## *STEPS TO TAKE IF YOU ARE IN DIRE FINANCIAL STRAITS*

1. Lock up your checkbook. This is the cardinal rule turnaround specialists follow when restructuring a troubled company. Pay only essential expenses such as rent, utility and loan payments. Use the remaining funds to extinguish debt or clear up other financial problems.

2. Eliminate all unnecessary out of pocket expenses. Spend money on the bare essentials such as food, commutation, and personal hygiene costs.

3. Stop using credit cards. On the one hand, if you are experiencing a severe cash crunch, credit cards provide a method of deferring payment and thereby create cash. On the other hand, some day those credit card bills must be paid along with high interest. If you are in financial trouble, stop spending money on credit cards. Use your money (except savings) to reduce credit card debt.

4. Eat home and bring your lunch to work. The savings can be enormous. And, save the leftovers for another meal.

5. Stop buying luxury items and anything else you don't need. These may include tickets to concerts and theater, records and compact discs, clothes and vacations.

6. Stay home. Although this can be boring, an evening at home can be very enjoyable and almost always costs less than going to your favorite restaurant and disco. Rent a video tape, play "Trivial Pursuit" or "Monopoly" (board games), or borrow a book from the library.

7. Get a second and perhaps third job. This should occupy all your time and prevent you from spending money. Some jobs provide meals, and this can be a significant savings. Also, the extra income (cash flow) should alleviate your financial trouble.

8. Get a roommate to reduce your housing costs. Roommate services will help to screen any boarders. If it becomes impossible to make ends meet, consider terminating your lease and moving in with relatives.

9. Borrow money from your family.

10. Only as a last resort, sell something you own but don't need. Use this tactic with extreme caution because it is difficult or even impossible to buy back your possessions. If you are in financial trouble, you may be desperate and under stress, and selling your possessions may make you even more upset. The other problem is that the items people would pay the most for are the items you want to keep. But, if you there are no other sources of cash, you may have to sell something. And, if you do take this route, try to avoid pawn shops.

## *OTHER BUDGETING TIPS*

1. Manage paying large periodic expenditures. Suppose your auto insurance is due in April. Limit your credit card usage in February and March and your April credit card bill should be relatively low. Paying the insurance should be no problem.

2. Seasonal jobs. Suppose Jack quits his old job and lands a seasonal job where his employer pays him during the ten months he works. Jack receives 10 checks during September through June and none in July and August. Jack's annual salary $30,000, and his tax rate is 30%, so he takes home $21,000 ($30,000 minus $9,000 in taxes).

   Jack's best strategy is to spend only part of his salary every pay period to avoid a cash crunch during the months when he will not receive a check (July and August). Calculate the amount he should spend every month with this formula:

   Annual take home pay (salary minus income taxes)
   divided by 12 months per year.

   Jack should spend $1,750 every month ($30,000 annual salary minus $9,000 of income taxes divided by 12 months per year). If Jack spends $1,750 and saves $350 every month in which receives a check, he should be able to spend $1,750 during July and August when he receives no checks.

3. Spend less. This sounds obvious, but consider this example. Recently, my friend Floyd wanted to buy the new top-of-the-line Ford Explorer which costs approximately $30,000. A dealer offered him a five-year loan at 10% interest rate; the monthly payments equalled $637.41. As much as Floyd wanted the Explorer, he decided he couldn't afford it. He bought a Honda which costs $12,000 and the dealer offered him a loan with the same terms; the monthly payments equal $254.96. Floyd could afford the less expensive car and still manage to take a great vacation this year without going into debt.

4. If you have many large periodic expenses which occur in various months throughout the year, it can be helpful to complete a monthly budget. Such expenditures include car insurance and tax payments. Take out scrap paper and make 12 columns; label each one January through December. Make categories and plan your spending accordingly in order to meet those payments.

5. Compare your budget with your actual spending. Review the budget you prepared in Worksheet III with your cash outflows per your bank and credit card statements to see where you deviated from your plan. Use your actual spending experience to plan your budget for the upcoming year.

6. Get a second job during your peak spending times. Suppose you go shopping every Saturday afternoon and typically spend $100 at the mall. If you landed a Saturday-afternoon job, you would avoid spending money at the stores and earn money: a double bonus.

7. Set up an automatic withdrawal program to attain short term financial goals. Mutual fund companies will gladly withdraw your budgeted savings amount from your checking or savings account every month (this tactic is discussed more fully in the section Wealth Building Strategies). While most people use this program to facilitate their long term saving, this concept can be applied to short term savings.

   Suppose you want to save $1,200 this year for your vacation. This means you must save $100 every month in order to accumulate $1,200 by year end. After reviewing your budget and your checkbook, you notice that your checking account balance is low and you conclude you have difficulty setting aside money regularly to save for vacation. Upon contacting a mutual fund company, you learn they will wire transfer money every month from your checking account to their mutual fund. And, if you save $100 every month, at the end of the year, you should accumulate $1,200 plus interest income. One mutual fund company, Twentieth Century Investors (1-800-345-2021) has such a program and will withdraw as little as $25 from your checking account every month; currently Twentieth Century deducts expenses from the fund income and charges an annual $10 account maintenance fee for accounts with balances below $1,000.

   (a) Why set up this program? It is difficult to set aside money every month. This tactic makes the money disappear from your checking account automatically, every month, and since you cannot spend the money, you are forced to save for vacation. When you go on vacation you will avoid paying your credit card company so much interest.

   (b) What is the best investment to make? A money market investment which invests in conservative safe investments such as Treasury bills, bank CDs and short-term A-rated corporate obligations. Since you need the money in a relatively short time period, you want to preserve your principal investment.

8. The best strategy for financial success is live within your means and avoid incurring massive credit card debt. Then wealth-building will be easy.

## *WORKSHEET IV - PRESENT VALUE (Today's Value of Money)*

**(to be used in conjunction with Financial Table I).**

Suppose Jack's grandparents decide to help him buy his dream house and are willing to give him a gift which would enable him to make the $7,200 down payment in 1995. To figure out how much money Jack's grandparents must give him today, Jack has to calculate the present value of $7,200 he needs four years from today. Present value is the amount of money one has today or the value today, of money one expects to receive in the future.

Turn to Worksheet IV (page 97) to calculate the present value (amount needed today) of money received/needed in the future.

1. The first column is labelled, "Years"; enter the number of years in your time horizon. Jack has 4 years to attain his goal.

2. Suppose Jack locates a risk-free investment which pays interest at the rate of 7%. Enter the rate (7%) in the column titled "Interest Rate".

   If you can invest money at a fractional rate of interest (7.8% for example), choose the factor in the column with the lower interest rate (7.0% in this example).

3. To find the correct financial factor, turn to Financial Table I, the Present Value of $1 (page 102) and locate the factor corresponding to 4 years and 7%. Since Jack has a 4 year time horizon, he should move down the left-most column which is marked years to the row marked "4" years. The other columns correspond to interest rates. Move across the table from left to right along the row marked "4", and stop at the column labelled "7.00%". The proper present value factor is located where the row (4 years) meets the column (7%), and equals 0.7564. Enter the correct financial factor from Financial Table I in the third column on Worksheet IV labelled "Factor".

4. Use the fourth column for the "Final Amount" (which in Jack's case is the $7,200 down-payment in 1995). Remember, this is the amount needed to attain your financial goal.

5. To calculate the present value, multiply the Factor in column 3 by the "Final Amount" in column 4. The present value equals $5,446.08 (0.7564 multiplied by $7,200) assuming Jack can invest his money at 7% or more continually and he leaves all the money on deposit to grow (e.g. Jack pays all taxes from his salary). Jack's grandparents should give him $5,446.08 in order to accumulate the $7,200 by 1995.

Alternatively, if Jack could invest his money in an account which pays 10%, his grandparents should give him $4,834.80 (see example 2 in Worksheet IV). Following the second example in Worksheet IV, Jack has 4 years and 10% interest rate; the factor equals 0.6715; the final amount equals $7,200. The present value equals $4,834.80. Notice that the amount of money Jack's grandparents must give Jack drops to $4,834.80; this is because the bank pays higher interest rates. If interest rates were lower than the 7% in the original example, Jack's grandparents would have to deposit more than $5,446.08 in his account.

## *WORKSHEET V - FUTURE VALUE (Tomorrow's Value of Money)*

**(to be used in conjunction with Financial Table II).**

Alternatively, suppose Jack has $500 today (the principal or present value) and can deposit the money in a Certificate of Deposit (CD) which earns 6% interest every year. Let's figure out how much the $500 will grow to (compound or future value) in four years when Jack wants to buy his condo. To calculate the amount of money Jack expects to accumulate at the end of four years, use the future value formula in Worksheet V (page 98).

1. The first column is labelled, "Years"; enter the number of years before your goal. Jack has 4 years in which the money can grow.

2. Enter the rate (6%) in the next column. If you assume an interest rate, make sure you can invest at that rate or higher continuously throughout the entire investment horizon. Generally, short-term investments pay lower rates than longer-term ones, and if you invest money every year, the rates may decline and you will have to save more money every month in order to achieve your goal.

   If you can invest money at a fractional rate of interest (5.6% for example), choose the factor in the column with the lower interest rate (5.0% in this example).

3. To find the correct financial factor, turn to Financial Table II, the Future Value of $1 (page 103). Since Jack has a 4 year time horizon, he should choose the appropriate factor in the row marked "4 years". Moving across the table from left to right along the row marked "4", stop at the column labelled "6.00%". The proper future value factor equals 1.2704. Enter the correct financial factor from Financial Table II in the third column on Worksheet V labelled "Factor".

4. Use the fourth column for the "Present Value" (the amount of money in hand today), which in Jack's case, is $500.

5. To calculate the future value, multiply the Factor in column 3 by the "Present Value" in column 4. The future value equals $635.20 ($500 multiplied by 1.2704). Remember, this factor assumes Jack can invest his money at 6% or more every year and he leaves all the money on deposit to grow. If Jack withdraws money to pay income taxes for example, the future value will be less than $635.20.

Recall that Jack's grandparents were willing to give him a gift of $5,446.08 today assuming Jack could invest the money at 7% until 1995. Now that Jack should have $635.20 in his bank account by 1995, granddad figures he could give Jack less than $5,446.08. The $500 Jack already has should grow to $635.20 by 1995, and Jack should need only $6,564.80 ($7,200 minus $635.20) more to make the $7,200 down payment in 1995.

Returning to Worksheet IV (page 97), the Present Value of $1 (line 3), assume Jack's grandparents can take advantage of the 7% rate for 4 years. The factor equals: 0.7564. The "Final Amount" equals $6,564.80. So, Jack's grandparents should give him $4,965.61. If Jack doesn't squander his money and forecasted interest rates (6%) hold true, the $500 today should grow to $635.20, and the $4,965.61 today should grow to $6,564.80 (if invested at 7%); then Jack should have $7,200 ($635.20 plus $6,564.80) in four years.

Note: The fact that the investments pay different interest rates can be confusing. You can add or subtract money at the same point in time (paid or received on the same date) because the money has the same value in time: $1 received today equals $1 today. When the investment rates differ, consider the present value (future value) of each investment separately and calculate the future value (present value) separately based on the applicable interest rates. Once you calculate both future values (present values), you can add or subtract the monies because they will be received at the same point in time.

## *WORKSHEET VI - MONTHLY DEPOSITS (Annuities)*

**(to be used in conjunction with Financial Table III).**

Suppose Jack has a fight with his grandparents before they sign the check, and they decide to forego the gift. Now Jack has to raise the $7,200 on his own.

Jack still has the $500 today which he can invest at 6% which should grow to $635.20 in four years, but he will be short by $6,564.80 ($7,200 minus $635.20).

Absent winning the lottery or inheriting the money, there is no reason why Jack should expect to suddenly come upon the money. If Jack is sensible and is serious about attaining his goal, he should establish a plan to deposit money every month in his savings account to accumulate the $6,565. A level payment which occurs periodically, such as every month, is called an annuity.

Use the Present Value Annuity formula in Worksheet VI (page 99) to calculate the monthly deposit needed to accumulate the $6,565 in the future.

1. The first column is labelled, "Years"; enter the number of years before your goal; Jack can save money for 4 years before his goal.

2. Since Jack is investing on a short-term basis, his bank pays only 5% interest on his money. Enter the rate (5%) in the column titled "Interest Rate". If you assume an interest rate, make sure you can invest at that rate (or higher) continuously throughout the entire investment horizon. Generally, short-term investments pay lower rates than longer-term ones, and if you invest money every year, the rates may decline and you will have to save more money every month in order to achieve your goal.

   If you can invest money at a fractional rate of interest (8.6% for example), choose the factor in the column with the lower interest rate (8.0% in this example).

3. To find the correct financial factor, turn to Financial Table III, the Monthly Annuity Amount to Accumulate $1 (page 104). Since Jack has a 4 year time horizon, he should choose the appropriate factor in the row marked "4 years". Moving across the table from left to right along the row marked "4", he should stop at the column labelled "5.00%". The proper present value factor equals 0.0189. Enter the correct financial factor from Financial Table III in the third column in Worksheet VI labelled "Factor".

4. Use the fourth column for the "Final Amount" which, in Jack's case, is $6,565.

5. To calculate the monthly annuity amount, multiply the Factor in column 3 by the "Final Amount" in column 4. The monthly deposit amount equals $124.08 (round up to $125). Again, this assumes Jack will deposit this money by the end of every month in a separate savings account which pays at least 5% interest per year and will pay any income tax due out of his salary, leaving the money on deposit to earn interest (compound). Remember the higher the interest rates, the more interest income you should earn on a given monthly deposit, and the earlier you deposit your money in the bank, the more time there is to earn interest income.

Return to Worksheet III (pages 15 and 33) where Jack created his financial plan. Compare this monthly deposit of $125 with his proposed budget and see if he can achieve this goal. Saving $125 every month may be over-ambitious, and Jack may have to adjust his goals or time horizon. Better yet, he could get a second job, and implement the 82 Strategies to Save Money.

## *WORKSHEET VII - FUTURE VALUE of MONTHLY DEPOSITS (Annuities)*
**(to be used in conjunction with Financial Table IV).**

The prior discussion of annuities (Monthly Deposits - Annuities; Worksheet VI), assumes you have a financial target in mind and want to calculate the monthly deposit necessary to accumulate the target amount of money. This section (Worksheet VII - page 100) assumes you deposit a certain amount in a savings account by the end of every month and want to calculate how much you should accumulate at the end of a number of years.

Suppose Jack reviews his budget (Worksheet III - page 15) and cannot afford to deposit $125 every month. Maybe saving $100 or $75 is feasible. To calculate the amount of money his 4 years of monthly deposits should grow to at the end of four years, use the future value of an annuity formula in Worksheet VII (page 100).

Jack decides to deposit $75 in his savings account every month for four years; the bank pays 5% interest. Note: instead, Jack could deposit $75 in his account for six years and buy his condominium in 1997 instead of 1995.

1. The first column is labelled, "Years"; enter the number of years before your goal. Jack has 4 years.

2. Since Jack invests money on a short-term basis, a bank pays only 5% interest. Enter the rate (5%) in the second column. Make sure you can invest money at the rate (or a higher rate) you used to calculate your monthly savings amount or higher.

   If you can invest money at a fractional rate of interest (8.3% for example), choose the factor in the column with the lower interest rate (8.0% in this example).

3. To find the correct financial factor, turn to Financial Table IV, the Future Value of Monthly Deposits (page 105). Since Jack has a 4 year time horizon, he should choose the appropriate factor in the row marked "4 years". Moving across the table from left to right along the row marked "4", he should stop at the column labelled "5.00%". The proper future value factor equals 53.0148. Enter the correct financial factor from Financial Table IV in the third column on Worksheet VII labelled "Factor".

4. Use the fourth column for the "Monthly Deposit" (the amount of money Jack plans to deposit every month) or $75.

5. To calculate the future value of 4 years worth of monthly deposits, multiply the Factor in column 3 by the "Monthly Deposit" in column 4. The future value (the amount of money Jack should have in four years) equals $3,976.11. Remember, this factor assumes Jack makes the deposit every month and can invest his money at 5% or more every year; if he withdraws money or interest rates decline, the future value will drop.

   If Jack deposits $75 in his special savings account every month for 4 years and earns 5% interest, in 1995 he should have $3,976.11. Add the $635.20 (the future value of $500 invested today for 4 years at 6%), and Jack should have a total of $4,611.31 in 1995. But, since Jack needs $7,200 to make the down payment, he has a shortfall of $2,588.69 ($7,200 minus $4,611.31) or $2,589 rounded to the nearest dollar.

## *WORKSHEET VIII - MAKING UP THE SHORTFALL*

**(Pre-tax versus After-tax Money)**

The key to any shortfall or obstacle is to focus on the goal and not let the shortfall block your progress. There are dozens of ways for Jack to make up the shortfall; perhaps the easiest is getting a second job to earn the $2,589. But, to plan a complete financial strategy, Jack must differentiate between pre-tax and after-tax dollars. The $2,589 shortfall is in after-tax dollars, because Jack must accumulate that amount in order to write a check for the down payment. To earn $2,589 in after-tax dollars, Jack must earn more than $2,589 in pre-tax dollars. A salary goal is in pre-tax dollars.

Jack's annual salary of $30,000 is a pre-tax number, and Uncle Sam charges income taxes on that money. Since Jack's tax rate equals 30%, he pays $9,000 ($30,000 multiplied by 30%) in taxes; therefore, he takes home only $21,000.

Worksheet VIII (page 101) shows how to calculate the amount of pre-tax salary needed to arrive at an after-tax goal.

1. Enter your take-home pay in column 1 labelled: "Take-Home Pay". This should be the amount of money you deposit in your checking account every pay-period. Suppose Jack receives 24 pay-checks every year; therefore, he deposits $875 ($21,000 divided by 24) in his checking account twice a month.

2. Enter your gross salary in column 2 labelled: "Gross Salary". In Jack's case, he would earn $1,250 ($30,000 gross salary divided by 24 pay periods per year) twice a month.

3. Divide column 1 by column 2. Jack would divide $875 by $1,250 and find that he takes home 70% or 0.70 of every dollar of pre-tax salary he earns.

   Alternatively, Jack pays $375 in taxes every pay period. His tax rate equals 30% or 0.30 ($375 in taxes divided by $1,250 in gross salary). To figure out how much of Jack's dollar of salary he keeps after taxes, Jack should perform the following computation: 1.00 minus the tax rate equals the percentage take-home pay. In this case, 1.00 minus 0.30 equals 0.70 (or 100% minus 30% equals 70%). In either case, Jack would enter 0.70 in column 3.

4. Enter your <u>after-tax</u> financial goal in column 4. Jack's goal is $2,589.

5. Divide the after-tax financial goal in column 4 by the take-home pay percentage in column 3. Jack would divide $2,589 by 0.70; the answer is $3,698.57, and is the pre-tax or gross salary needed to accumulate $2,589 after-tax. Therefore, Jack should earn $3,698.57 or $3,700 in pre-tax dollars to achieve his goal.

6. Enter the amount of money you could earn per day in his second job. Jack can land a job which pays $50 per day, so he enters $50 in column 6.

7. Divide the pre-tax goal in column 5 by the salary per day in column 6. Jack would divide $3,698.57 by $50 dollars per day. In effect, he would have to work 73.97 or 74 days to make up the $2,589 after-tax shortfall.

   Jack has to work 74 days and earn $50 per day in order to earn $3,700.00 ($50 per day multiplied by 74 days) before tax. If Jack is in the 30% tax bracket, he will earn $2,590 ($3,700 multiplied by 70%) after tax. The second job provides enough money to make the down-payment.

You may also save money by trimming expenditures, and this is a proven and excellent strategy. Definitely continue pursuing this plan. However, raising your income level by landing a second job or securing a raise has a much greater impact on your ability to save money than trimming your expenses. For example, Jack earns $21,000 after-tax annually and if he has no living expenses, the amount of money he can save this year is limited to his take-home pay ($21,000) plus interest income. Suppose Jack lands a second job which pays $10,000 this year; Jack might be able to save $31,000 ($21,000 plus $10,000).

*The amount of money you can save*
*is limited by*
*the amount of your income minus your expenses.*

## *WEALTH - BUILDING STRATEGIES*

1. Establish a separate account for savings. Never commingle your daily spending money with your long-term savings because you will lose track of your money and inevitably deplete your savings. A separate savings account makes it difficult to withdraw money from the account and facilitates accumulating wealth. It is often helpful to establish your separate account with a mutual fund, brokerage house, or commercial bank which is separate from your daily bank.

2. Once you deposit money into your savings account, don't withdraw the money. Withdraw the money if your have an absolute hardship such as a medical emergency, or withdraw the money only when you are ready to buy your dream house or business. If you withdraw money from your wealth-building accounts, your bank balances will decline and you will never earn interest income.

3. Keep all your money in an interest-bearing account. Keep your money in a savings or money market account which pays interest income. Banks offer savings and checking accounts, and linking all your accounts together will enable you to transfer money from one account to another with the use of your bank card. When you write checks, be sure to transfer enough money from savings to checking so the checks won't bounce.

   One sound plan is: use a checking account for weekly spending and paying bills; use a savings account to save money for short term purposes such as vacations or purchasing clothes, and use a mutual fund for longer-term savings.

4. Sign up for direct deposit payroll service. If you deposit your check manually, the bank must clear the check which may take three days. With direct deposit, your employer wire transfers your pay check into your checking account on pay-day, and the funds are available immediately (generally, to take advantage of this service, you must maintain a checking account at your employer's bank).

   Through direct deposit payroll service, your money becomes available immediately (approximately three days earlier or more) every pay-period because the money is deposited in your account as cash. With the extra time, you can use the funds or invest the money and earn incremental interest income every year. With this strategy, you've made your money work for you and just created interest income for yourself with minimal effort.

   In addition, with direct deposit payroll service, you save the time and hassle of waiting on line at the bank to deposit your pay check every week.

5. Get free checking. Often, your company's commercial bank offers free checking to company employees. If you can take advantage of this benefit, you will save the monthly check charges. For example, if you currently pay $10 per month in check fees and service charges, you just created $120 per year, ($10 per month multiplied by 12 months per year). And the savings is in after-tax dollars.

6. Take advantage of compound interest. The bank pays you interest on interest. Your money accumulates geometrically instead of arithmetically.

   For example, Jack deposits $100 in a bank account that pays 10% per year. If the bank paid simple interest, he would earn 10% or $10 on the $100 every year. At the end of 25 years, the balance in his account would equal $350 (25 years multiplied by $100 deposit multiplied by 10% plus the original $100 deposit).

   Instead, suppose Jack deposit the $100 in a bank account that pays 10% interest compounded annually. This means he should earn $10 ($100 on deposit multiplied by 10%) in the first year and then in the second year, the bank pays interest on the new balance of $110 ($100 original deposit plus $10 interest); he earns $11 in the second year, and so on. At the end of 25 years, the balance would equal $1,083, quite a difference.

*Look for savings and interest-bearing checking accounts*
*which pay interest compounded daily or continuously.*
*And, leave your principal and interest on deposit,*
*and your wealth will grow very quickly.*

7. Pay all income taxes on investment income from your salary and leave your savings intact to grow. Unfortunately, the income taxes Uncle Sam charges on investment income hinder your wealth building. Suppose you withdraw money from your wealth-building account to pay income taxes; your bank account balance will drop and you will build less wealth. Use your salary to pay income taxes and you will accelerate your wealth-building. Similarly, reinvest all dividends from mutual funds.

8. When you receive a raise at work, don't spend it all. When you receive a raise, you could conclude the increase is a small amount, and there is no reason to bother saving the money. On the other hand, you could conclude that spending the money would not result in a great change in lifestyle so you could decide to save the money and accumulate wealth. A third strategy entails spending part of the raise and saving the remainder. The choice is yours.

9. Set up an automatic monthly savings plan. Mutual fund companies will gladly withdraw your budgeted savings amount from your checking account every month and deposit the money in your chosen mutual fund. As a result, you are forced to save money because your savings budget disappears from your checking account. Since you save money regularly, you should earn more investment income.

10. Open an interest-bearing checking account. Most banks offer checking accounts (often called NOW accounts) which pay interest on your average balance. You earn interest until your checks clear or you withdraw cash. It's possible to earn at least $25 to $50 annually; this is free money.

    Banks generally charge a flat monthly fee for this service and waive the monthly fee if you maintain a minimum balance (the minimum balance requirement is generally several thousand dollars). If the cost of the service (meeting the minimum deposit requirements or the monthly fee) exceeds the interest income you will earn, don't sign up. The cost of this service varies among banks so shop around for the best deal.

11. Generally, it is best to pay off debt with the highest interest rate first. If your credit card debt bears 20% interest and your student loans charge 11%, drag out the student loan payments for as long as possible in order to pay off the 20% debt first. Also, consult a CPA before paying off any loans to determine whether the interest expense is tax-deductible.

12. Open an IRA, Keogh or 401K plan. These plans are tax-deferred retirement plans where your contributions are deducted from your current annual taxable income and the income accumulates tax-free until you withdraw the money. Jack earns $30,000 every year, and if he deposits $2,000 in his 401K plan, he should pay income tax this year on only $28,000 ($30,000 minus $2,000). There are certain restrictions on deposits and withdrawals, and there are penalties associated with withdrawals under certain circumstances. Your money earns income tax-free, but withdrawals are generally taxed as ordinary income in the year of withdrawal.

    My company awards each employee an annual bonus of 3% of their salary, and if the employee leaves the money on deposit in the 401K plan, the company matches the 3% with another 3% award. This means that every year, eligible employees can earn 6% of their salary tax-free to save for retirement. If your company makes contributions to your 401K or other retirement plan, consider the money as money for your retirement. And, if there is a matching award program, take advantage of it; consider the money as extra money and leave it on deposit in the plan to grow.

13. Winning the Lottery or Inheriting Money. If you suddenly receive a large sum of money, don't change your lifestyle. Rather, pay off your debts (especially credit card debt), take a nice vacation, and perhaps buy a new car. Invest the majority of the money in a high quality mutual fund and spend only the dividends or interest income every year. Then you should have a higher standard of living for the rest of your life.

14. Even if you are burdened by thousands of dollars of debt, budget some money, $25, $50, or $100 to save every month. Then you will build wealth.

15. Never deplete your savings. Even if you are loaded with debts, don't wipe out your savings to pay off your debts. It is nearly impossible to rebuild savings because it is difficult to trim your spending habits to spend only the money you make, let alone less in order to pay off your debts. Besides, it is much more compelling to pay off money you owe to a bank or credit card company than to yourself. If you pay off your debts with your current salary, and leave your assets intact to grow, when you finally eliminate your debt, you will have accumulated wealth.

## *INVESTING MONEY*

Almost everyone I know wants to become wealthy, but few people take the steps necessary to build wealth. First, it is essential to budget and save a certain amount of money every month. Second, put your money to work: make investments to earn interest, dividends, and capital gains. Third, keep your money intact: don't make withdrawals for vacations, clothing purchases, or tax payments.

*Money Management is No Joke.*
*Your Wealth is at Stake.*
*So, Take Investing Money Very Seriously.*

Understand the distinction between individual investors (you and me) and institutional investors (big money - pensions, investment banks). Institutional money managers have an incredible edge over individual investors because the institutions move vast sums of money, pay little commissions, and have access to superior information. In short, the vast majority of people who invest in individual securities (stocks and bonds of specific companies), lose money. Suppose only 25 investors out of 100 investors make money in the stock market; that's not very good odds. If you have limited knowledge of investments and do not wish to master the subject, don't increase your chances of losing money. Rather, invest in high quality mutual funds.

The first and perhaps most important concept regarding investing money is determining whether you should choose your own investments or you should entrust your money to professional mutual fund managers. Thousands of different investment products exist, and many have different objectives. Further, many investors have difficulty choosing the optimal investment. The following questions should help you determine whether you should invest in specific securities (common stocks or bonds of specific corporations) or mutual funds. If you answer "NO" to any of the following questions, you are among the majority of people in this country and should invest in high-quality mutual funds.

1. Do you have the skills and knowledge to make profitable investments?

2. Do you have the time and desire to manage your investments and follow the stock market and current business events? On a daily basis?

3. If you don't have the time to learn about investing now, do you have the inclination and power to make the time?

**Rules of Investing Money**

Here are a few investment tips I have observed over the years. These ideas are by no means the last word on investing, and should be contemplated in light of many other factors, not the least of which are your own investing experience and sound financial advice from the appropriate financial advisor.

1. Ignore most of what you hear. No one knows everything about the market. And, the person at the cocktail party who brags about his huge stock market profits probably has at least as many losses.

2. Stock brokers don't know everything so don't automatically buy or sell stock based on your broker's advice. If your broker could predict the stock market, he would trade his own money instead of yours. In addition, stock brokers often have poor information, and too few brokers follow the business press. Further, brokers are influenced by their firm's research analysts who maintain a recommended list, and often, the brokers earn bonuses by selling stocks off the recommended list.

3. Don't trade excessively. Stock brokers are paid commissions based on the number of trades their customers make; therefore, the more times you buy and sell stock, the more commissions (money) your broker makes. It is in the broker's best interest for you to continually buy and sell stocks. Save commission charges; invest for the long run.

4. Never give your stock broker power of attorney. Many investors have lost substantial amounts of money because the broker decides which investments they will buy for you, and the broker may churn your account. The broker can end up with high commissions, and the investors have depleted their wealth. Instead, invest in a high quality mutual fund.

5. Scrutinize investment products created or sponsored by the brokerage house. These investments may be losers. Often, stock brokers encourage investors to buy the house products because the commission is higher than the commissions on other equivalent products. Further, investments with complex payout formulas and extensive restrictions (when and under what circumstances you can withdraw your money) may be dangerous.

6. Ignore cold calls. When stock brokers look for new accounts, they open the local telephone book and start dialing. Hang up on any stock broker who urges you to buy common stock over the telephone.

7. Choose a discount broker if you actively manage your money, decide which investments to make, and don't want a stock broker's advice. Discount brokers do not call to persuade you to buy stock, and the commissions should be significantly lower than those of a full-service firm. As of this printing, the least expensive firm I know of is Pacific Brokerage Services based in Los Angeles (1-213-939-1100).

8. Stick with areas you know. People have a lot more insight into industries they understand versus other industries. Suppose your hobby is computers and you follow the trade magazines; you know the new products hitting the market and should be able to make well-informed investment decisions regarding computer company stocks than companies in other industries. But don't assume you'll always make money investing in companies you are familiar with or that stock prices of companies in industries you are familiar with, will consistently rise.

9. If you don't know, ask. Recently, many research analysts have been recommending the big three auto manufacturers. I liked one company and wanted to know how they were faring. I visited a local car dealership, and a salesman explained the company's cars were not selling well. I passed on the investment.

10. Learn about the industry and companies before you invest, even if your broker tells you to buy a stock today. The New York Stock Exchange is closed only 7 days (aside from weekends) during the year so you have plenty of days in which to buy stock. Although timing is very important with respect to investing money, never rush into an investment; it is better to miss an opportunity than to lose your money.

11. If your initial strategy was wrong, close out the losers and move on to the next investment. When some investors lose 5% or 10% of their original investment, they sell out. On the other hand, if you have a solid long-term strategy and a stock declines in the short term, you will not necessarily lose money over the long run. Maybe it is time to buy more shares and lower your average cost. If you did make a mistake, get out.

12. It is better to sell too early than too late. If your industry and market knowledge tell you a company (stock) is on the way to the doghouse, sell out. Take your profit or minimize your losses, and find a more promising investment.

13. Let the winners ride. All of us get excited when we make a profit in the stock market, and we often take the money and run. This is okay because it is better to make money than to lose money. However, if you bought a common stock as a long term investment and you think the company's prospects are still strong, stick with the company.

14. Buy low, sell high. This is the most overused statement on Wall Street, but it makes sense. How about, "Buy high, sell higher"? That phrase has been around the block almost as many times as the first expression, but in a rising market, this can be a profitable strategy. If your knowledge and instinct tell you a stock is headed north, buy the stock.

15. Don't buy stocks on margin. Customers who buy stocks on margin borrow money from the brokerage house. Suppose you have $1,000 to invest. If the margin requirement (cash down payment percentage) equals 50% of the investment, your broker may say, "Give me the $1,000, and the brokerage house will lend you another $1,000. Then you can buy double the number of shares and double your profit." First, you own twice as many shares. Second, the broker earns a higher commission. Third, you will double your profits, and double your losses. Fourth, regardless of the outcome, you owe the brokerage house the money you borrowed, plus interest.

16. Be wary of "Hot Tips." Often, insiders create "hot tips" or rumors because they want to sell out to the public. Suppose a company is headed for trouble; if insiders create positive rumors, individual investors may rush into the market to buy the shares. Eventually, the buying pressure stops and the stock price falls. Avoid get-rich-quick investments, and invest for the long term.

17. Above-market yields often signal INCREASED RISK. Your investment is really a company's borrowing. When a bank or brokerage house sells a Certificate of Deposit, the financial institution in effect borrows money from the investors, and there are few if any, restrictions on what the financial institution can use the money for. Similarly, when a mutual fund sells shares in a common stock fund, the fund sponsor borrows money from the investors and promises to invest the money in common stocks. With this in mind, it is important to assess the risks associated with making investments.

    Find out whether:

    a) your financial institution is creditworthy (financially strong).

    b) the financial institution is likely to exist when you want to redeem your money.

    c) your investment is likely to pay off (probability of earning a profit).

    There can be valid reasons why financial institutions offer above-average yields. When mutual fund companies open new funds, they sometimes offer above-market yields to attract investors. Reasonable yield differentials approximate 0.5% and usually arise because the mutual fund company reduces the management fees and expenses. Generally, these higher yields last for a limited time period. If you are comfortable with the sponsor's track record and reputation, and understand the nature of the investment, then the investment may be okay. But Read the prospectus (offering memorandum) before investing your money.

Investments which pay above-market rates of return generally bear significantly more risk. For example, investors who lend money to the U.S. government expect to receive both interest and principal, if only for the fact the government would tax the people to repay the loan.

On the other end of the spectrum, consider lending money to a company on the verge of bankruptcy. First, a rational investor wouldn't lend the money unless he was reasonably sure he would recover the new money or he had to lend the new money to recover the money he previously lent. Second, if the investor decided to lend the new money, he would charge a higher interest rate as compensation for accepting increased risk (the chance the company might declare bankruptcy, and he would lose both his principal and interest).

Financial institutions sometimes offer higher yields because they are unable to borrow money from other sources. Beware of underlying financial problems which may increase your risk. Visit the public library and read the current news on the institution who is holding your wealth, or consult a financial advisor. Value Line, an investment publication available in any public library, provides thorough and timely information.

Although it may be somewhat difficult today, seek out a secure financial institution who will be in business when you want to redeem your money. Maintain accounts with banks that are FDIC (Federal Deposit Insurance Corp.) insured, and if you open a money market account with a brokerage house, choose an old-line, reputable company which is SIPC (Securities Investor Protection Corporation) insured. These insurance plans may preserve your money in the event the company goes bankrupt.

Don't be afraid of increased risk. Assuming more risk may be acceptable depending on your view of the nature and safety of the investment, your tolerance for risk, and the expected return on investment. Different people are comfortable accepting varying levels of risk. Generally, it is safer to take more risks when you are younger because you can recover from mistakes more easily than when you are older. And, to build wealth, it is usually necessary to invest in growth assets. So, consider investing some percentage of your wealth in growth investments which may bear more risk and will hopefully yield higher returns.

Remember, your goal is to build wealth, not deplete it. **If you are uncomfortable with an investment, pass.** You are much better off earning a conservative yield than losing your money. And, always gain an understanding of the investment and the potential risks and rewards before investing.

18. Compare the fees on one investment with those of comparable investments before investing money. Almost all investments bear fees in one form or another. If there are no fees, the investment sponsor may be trying to unload his holdings (almost a sure sign of trouble and a conflict of interest). Beware of investments which bear exorbitant fees in relation to the probable returns. Investment companies and financial advisors are in business to make money; accordingly, they charge fees and expenses which reduce your return on investment. Choose investments which yield good returns and charge reasonable fees.

    Last year, my Certificate of Deposit (CD) matured, and a salesperson encouraged me to invest in a common stock mutual fund. At the time, the stock market was relatively low and rising, so the investment seemed reasonable. After extolling the virtues of this stock fund, the salesperson reluctantly admitted there was an 8% sales charge to enter the fund. That meant that for every $100 I deposited, only $92 were working for me. And, that 8% sales charge was up-front in addition to annual fees and expenses. I found a suitable "No-Load" stock fund and avoided the heavy fees. By the way, the rates of return on the two funds were approximately equal over the time period.

    Limited Partnerships and other complex investments often charge management fees in excess of 10% per year. In addition, the general partners or investment managers often take a preferential return (profit) before the investors receive profit. Before you invest in these vehicles, analyze the business project, the likelihood of making a profit, the risks involved, and the nature and extent of the fees you will be charged. Don't be afraid to consult a trustworthy financial advisor who charges you by the hour or by the project.

    Mutual funds also charge varying fees. "No-Load" mutual funds charge annual management expenses but do not charge a commission when you deposit or withdraw money; further, there is no specific proof that "Load" funds earn higher rates of return than "No-Loads". Where possible, choose the "No-Load" fund.

19. Invest only with honest people. It is amazing how quickly money disappears when the investment managers are dishonest. Double-check any references you receive.

20. Make sure your money manager is compensated in the same way you are. If you invest in a mutual fund, find out whether the fund manager owns shares in the same fund. This way, he makes money when you do. And, in the event of a crisis, the investment manager has his money at stake, he is more likely to stick around to correct the situation.

21. If your gut instinct tells you an investment is bad, pass. Conduct your own research until you become comfortable with an investment. When you are ready, invest your money carefully, slowly, and confidently.

**Picking Winning Stocks**

1. Learn how to invest money. Five of my favorite books on investing money are:

   a) One Up on Wall Street by Peter Lynch, the former Fidelity Magellan mutual fund manager, published by Simon & Shuster. This book is very readable and informative.

   b) Graham & Dodd's Securities Analysis, Fifth Edition published by McGraw Hill; this edition has been updated and is still considered the bible of securities analysis. You will learn a lot, but the book is very technical.

   c) The Wall Street Waltz - 90 Visual Perspectives by Kenneth L. Fisher, Forbes magazine columnist. This book contains easy-to-read charts about financial cycles and trends.

   d) Quality of Earnings by Thornton O'Glove explains how to analyze annual reports and differentiate between the core, sustainable earnings and the one-time gains.

   e) How to Read Annual Reports Intelligently - A Stockholder's Guide, by Adolph Lurie. This book is comprehensive yet easy to read and understand.

2. Follow the stock market and current events every day.

   a) Read the Wall Street Journal (1-800-628-9320) or the business section of a national newspaper such as the New York Times (1-800-631-2500), **every day**.

   b) Subscribe to BusinessWeek (212-512-2000) and Forbes (212-620-2200) magazines; these are my two favorite magazines. You will learn about a wide variety of industries, companies and business topics.

   c) Subscribe to Money magazine (1-800-633-9970). This monthly provides information on personal finance: taxes, investing money, mortgage rates, and Certificates of Deposit (CD) rates.

3. Read The Value Line Investment Survey ("Value Line") before investing any money. Digest the industry discussion and the analyses of each company within an industry group, and you should be able to make a more informed investment decision. The Value Line analysts update the industry and company reports at least four times per year. This publication is available in most public libraries. Reading Value Line before investing money has saved me thousands of dollars.

4. Form a network of people to discuss economics and the stock market (but always filter the information).

5. Use your common sense. If a business strategy seems impossible or nearly impossible to execute, it probably is.

6. Discover the industry's prospects. Look for industries with continuing upward trends. This is simple, but few investors take the time to determine whether their target industry has high growth prospects and the nature of emerging trends. If you read enough about industries and companies, the trends should become clear. After determining the major trends' affect on an investment, decide how to invest.

7. Discover the competitive forces in the industry. The competition includes other companies in the same industry; however, competitors emerge from far-off places. When I was an MBA student at Columbia University, my marketing professor, Morris Holbrook, PhD, offered two examples:

    1) Years ago, people used slidc rules to perform complex mathematical calculations. The slide rule industry competed vigorously to develop the most elaborate device. One day, someone invented the electronic calculator. How many people do you know who use a slide rule?

    2) The telefacsimile or fax machine enables people to transmit documents via telephone instantaneously. The US Postal Service had a virtual monopoly on non-bulk deliveries until Fred Smith founded Federal Express, the overnight package delivery service. Then, in the 1980's, most offices purchased a fax machine. Now, both the US Postal Service and Federal Express are suffering.

8. Observe the market for your company's and industry's products. For example, if you want to invest in consumer products companies, visit several supermarkets. Whose products control the shelves? Which companies offer the most products? Which products move the fastest? Who has the best brand recognition? Do the company's products work? Do the company's products fulfill customer needs? Do they add value?

    In the early 1980's, The Gap (Gap Stores Incorporated), the clothing store, made a tremendous turnaround. New stores were opening all over New York, and shoppers flocked out of the stores carrying bags full of Gap clothes. This was a good sign and warranted further research. Value Line recommended Gap, and the value of the shares has increased at least tenfold since then.

9. Learn the basic laws of Economics 101: Supply and Demand.

   a) When demand is high relative to supply, a company can charge high prices and reap great profits.

   b) In time, excess profits disappear because other companies enter the market and compete first on technological or service innovation, and later on price. Ultimately, companies in an industry sell basically the same products and the lowest priced product wins. And once price wars persist, company profits decline.

   Also, learn about macroeconomics and how government monetary policy influences the stock market.

10. Invest in companies who make value-added products. Commodity products compete on price, and price wars signal declining profits. But value-added products command premium prices.

11. Big companies tend to make more money. Large companies generally win over the long run because they can buy their way out of trouble. Often, the emerging company offers only one product, and their future depends on the success of that product whereas large companies have the resources to develop multiple product lines. This does not mean investors should avoid investing in growth companies because the US is an excellent country for entrepreneurship and some start-up companies make millions, and their stock prices increase twenty-fold.

12. How good is the company's management? If management's capabilities are low, your company is less likely to flourish.

13. Read the annual report carefully. Compare annual reports of different companies in an industry and for each company over several years. Does the chairman's letter vary from year to year? Generally positive signs include: news about capital expenditures, expansion plans (especially internationally because many countries outside the US are experiencing faster growth rates, and this translates into higher profits), and new products. One potentially negative sign is if the company's strategies change from year to year.

Also read the public accountant's opinion; as a rule, invest only in companies where the accountants gave an "unqualified opinion". I excerpted this unqualified opinion from a 1990 annual report (although the wording may be different):

> "In our opinion, the accompanying [financial statements] present fairly, in all material respects, the financial position of the Company...at December 31, 1990 and 1989, in conformity with generally accepted accounting principles..."

Analyze any exceptions carefully. Such exceptions include material events which effect the company's viability.

14. Choose companies which have a consistent record of paying dividends. Better yet, invest in companies which pay quarterly dividends that have grown continuously over time. This strategy does not contemplate growth companies who do not pay dividends; rather, they reinvest all the profits in the business.

15. Look for stocks with a dividend yield greater than 5%. The dividend yield is calculated by dividing the annual dividend by the current stock price. The yield is listed in the paper. For example, a company's dividend equals $0.80 per share and its current market price equals $7 per share. The dividend yield equals 11.4% ($0.80 divided by $7). Before buying a stock with a high dividend yield, be confident the company is in a temporary downturn and will recover. Companies who are in a slump experience cash shortages often reduce or eliminate the dividend. If the company can recover and will continue paying the dividend, the higher the yield, the better the value.

16. Look for stocks with price earnings (P-E) ratio less than 10 times. The P-E ratio is the market price of the stock divided by the latest year's earnings. Suppose XYZ company's forecasted earnings are $1.25 per share, and the current market price is $8 per share; the P-E ratio equals 6.4 times. Investors pay $6.40 for every dollar in earnings. The lower the P-E ratio, the better the value for a prospective buyer. But, be confident of the company's prospects.

17. Look for cash flow from operations which grows from year to year. If cash flow is falling, look out. Rising accounting earnings and earnings per share are terrific, but cash flow pays the bills and fuels expansion.

18. Look for low leverage (debt). Two measures of leverage are the debt to total capital ratio and the interest coverage ratio. The first shows how much the firm relies on debt to fund its operations; the more debt, the more risky the company. The second measures how many times the company can "cover" (pay) its interest bill based essentially on its profitability. The higher this ratio, the greater the financial strength of the company. Study the books listed above to learn more about financial ratios.

## A Brief Description of Several Popular Investments

The following is a **brief** description of some popular investments. You should not make any investment decisions based on these overviews. Keep in mind that every investment bears different risk and reward profiles and you should make investments which meet your financial goals. For example, the prices of stocks rise and fall so it is possible to lose money, and if you are risk averse, you may want to select another investment. As this is not a course in investing money and I am not a tax or investment advisor, you should consult your investment advisor before investing any money.

If you want to learn more about different investments, study these two books:

> Dun & Bradstreet's Guide to Your Investments (Harper & Row). This annual is very thorough and describes a wide variety of investments.
>
> Money Markets by Marcia Stigum is more technical but a great book.

1. Common Stocks represent ownership (equity) in corporations. Shares of common stock trade on organized stock exchanges (the New York Stock Exchange, the American Stock Exchange, or the Over-the-Counter Market). Generally, the companies listed (traded) on the New York Stock Exchange are the best capitalized companies (strongest financially, although they sometimes get into financial trouble). Also these companies are widely covered by the media.

   Investors buy common stocks to receive dividends (quarterly cash payments which the company will hopefully increase over time) and possible capital gains (appreciation - buy the stock at $10 per share and sell the stock at $20 per share; the capital gain equals $10 ($20 minus $10)). Investors risk losing their entire investment (the purchase price of the stock), but the upside return can be unlimited. Buying the right common stock can be very profitable.

2. Corporate Bonds are company IOU's. Companies borrow money from investors and promise to return the money (principal) plus interest.

   Investors buy bonds to receive semi-annual interest payments (coupons) and capital gains if the bonds are sold before maturity. Borrowers pay interest twice a year (semi-annual) and repay the principal at maturity (the end of a bond's life which might be 5 or 10 years). Bonds are issued in $1,000 (the face value) increments. Generally investors lend the borrower $1,000 (buy the bond for $1,000), and the borrower may pay a $50 coupon semi-annually (10% interest for example, multiplied by $1,000 (the face value) divided by 2 payment periods per year); if the investor holds a bond to maturity and the issuer is still solvent (financially secure), the investor should receive the face value ($1,000).

When market interest rates fall, the price of a bond rises. When market interest rates rise, the price of a bond falls. A bond's price moves in the opposite direction of the market yield (rate of return). A 10% bond is more valuable than an 8% bond because the $100 interest payments exceed the $80 investors will receive on new bonds. When market interest rates fall to 8%, the price of your 10% bond should rise until your bond yields 8% (absent any changes in creditworthiness) because investors should pay more and more money for a bond paying $100 per year until the yield matches the 8% market yield. Similarly, the prices of bonds with below-market yields should fall until the bond's yield equals the market yield.

Corporate bonds are rated for safety by Standard & Poor's (S&P) and Moody's Investor Service, among others. The S&P and Moody's ratings for investment grade bonds range from BBB to AAA and Baa to Aaa, respectively (AAA and Aaa are the highest). Generally, the lower a company's debt rating, the higher the interest rate they must pay investors; investors charge higher rates because there is more risk of losing money. Make investments to earn money, not lose it; therefore, purchase only investment grade bonds issued by high quality companies you know and like. Here are the investment-grade ratings:

| S & P | Moody's |
|---|---|
| AAA | Aaa |
| AA | Aa |
| A | A |
| BBB | Baa |

3. Junk Bonds. These bonds are rated below-investment grade. Some junk bond have investors made money, and many have lost money. Avoid junk bonds.

4. Government Bonds

   a) The US Federal government issues debt which is considered to be risk-free because Uncle Sam agrees to make good on the borrowing. The interest income on these instruments is usually exempt from state income taxes.

      i) Treasury bills mature in less than one year. T-bills are issued in $5,000 increments although the minimum investment is $10,000. These are discount notes because a $10,000 face value bond can be purchased for less than $10,000, and upon maturity, the Federal government repays $10,000. Stock brokers and banks will buy T-bills on your behalf for a nominal commission, or you can save the commission by opening your own account with the US Treasury Department (Bureau of Public Debt; Securities Transactions Branch; Room 2134; Main Treasury; Washington DC 20226).

ii) Treasury Notes are issued with maturities between one and ten years from date of issuance, and Treasury Bonds mature in more than ten years from the date of issuance.

b) State and local government bonds. The interest income on these bonds is generally exempt from Federal income taxes and often income taxes within the same state as well. The buying decision depends on the after-tax yield on these bonds compared with the after-tax yield on taxable bonds. Equally important is the financial health of the issuer, and these days, many municipalities are experiencing budget deficits. Some of these bonds are guaranteed by AMBAC or MBIA which makes them safer. Some state and local governments have defaulted on their bonds, so research the issuer's health before investing.

i) General Obligation Bonds are backed by the full faith and taxing power of a state or local government. These are often the safest bonds issued by a municipality.

ii) Revenue Bonds are backed by the income from a specific project such as a bridge or tunnel. The safety of these instruments depends on the success of the project.

5. The Government National Mortgage Association (GNMA) issues Ginnie Mae's (GNMA's) which are pools of home mortgages. These bonds are backed by GNMA, a Federal government agency, but are not directly guaranteed by the Federal government. These bonds typically pay attractive yields and are relatively safe investments. Investors should understand that when mortgage rates decline significantly, homeowners tend to refinance their mortgages at lower interest rates, and in that case, your GNMA may be called (before maturity), and then you would receive the outstanding balance of the underlying mortgage.

6. Options, Futures, and commodities generally bear significant risk and limited payoffs. People who trade these types of securities tend to buy and sell often; remember, the stock broker makes money on commissions when you buy and sell securities; you, on the other hand, may win or lose.

   Call options give the holder (owner) the right to buy shares of a common stock at a specified price for a set time period. And, at the end of the time period (put and call options are generally issued for terms of 3, 6, or 9 months) the put and call options expire.

Some brokers encourage their clients to buy put options as a form of insurance against declines in stock prices by giving the holder (owner) the right to sell shares of a common stock at a specified price for a set time period. Put options, like any other insurance policy, expire, and the insurance exists only as long as you continue to buy more put options. If you are convinced the price of your stock is about to fall, you are probably better off selling the stock. Trading options is very complex, and generally a waste of money because on average options expire worthless.

Other brokers recommend commodities (for example, corn, wheat, gold, and oil) whose prices are a function of the supply and demand for a crop or natural resource. Institutional traders control the commodities markets. A large percentage of the commodity trades protects a buyer's position (hedging). Hedging encompasses a strategy entirely different from the individual investor's goal which is speculation on price movements and crop yields. Most of the people I know who have invested in these products lost money. Don't trade commodities.

7. Troubled companies. Investing in common stocks or bonds of turnarounds can be very profitable, but it is crucial to understand the prospects for the company, the nature of the company's businesses, and management's capabilities. This is a high-risk game.

8. Coins and other collectibles. Buy them to enjoy them. High returns on investment are difficult to predict and sales commissions are high. There is no liquid market for coins and most other collectibles, so determining a fair price becomes difficult.

9. Selling a stock short. This means you sell shares of common stock you don't own. In effect you borrow one person's stock and sell the shares to a third party. At some point, you have to repurchase the shares in the open market and return them to the rightful owner. If you sell short ABC Company at $50 per share, an investor should pay you $50. If the price of ABC Company drops to $40 per share, you could repurchase the shares for $40 and make $10 profit (sell at $50 and buy at $40) on each share. Simple, right? The shares could just as easily soar to $65 per share, and you would lose $15 (sell at $50 and buy at $65) per share. The brokerage house also requires the investor to put money on deposit (margin) to protect against adverse price movements. Forget this scheme.

10. Certificates of Deposit (CDs). Banks and brokerage houses offer CDs for periods (maturities) ranging from three-months to five years and pay a stated, constant interest rate over that time period. These investments are as safe as the financial institution who issues them and can be a good investment when interest rates are high or investors seek a stated rate of return. Look for FDIC (Federal Deposit Insurance Corporation) insured banks or financially secure brokerage houses with an excellent track record and reputation.

11. <u>Initial Public Offerings (IPO)</u>. Companies "go public" (commencing trading on a national stock exchange) for a variety of reasons. Two common reasons are: 1) Owners/Founders want to cash out; 2) The company needs more money to grow.

    Some companies that go public are dynamos and the shareholders earn thousands of dollars, and other publicly traded companies go bankrupt. Make sure you read the entire prospectus (offering memorandum) carefully before investing and be sure that your investment will fuel expansion and not merely line the founder's pockets. Also, you must be very confident that the company has a sound strategy which management can execute. Reputable brokerage houses value their reputation and strive to issue only common stocks of high quality companies because the brokerage house looks bad if a large number of its IPO's fail.

    Often the public rushes to the market to buy shares of an IPO which drives up the price; the buying pressure may be short-lived and you may be able to buy the stock several weeks later for less money. Nonetheless, a hot IPO can be a winner.

12. <u>Penny Stocks</u>. These are shares of common stock which trade for a few cents or a few dollars per share. Often, these stocks are thinly traded, and wide price swings occur daily. There is often a scarcity of information about these companies, and lack of size and financial strength. Besides, to make a meaningful profit, you have to buy hundreds of shares of stock, and this puts a lot of your money at risk. Generally, avoid these investments.

13. <u>Real Estate</u> can be a good investment if the cash flow from rent exceeds expenses, and the property is fairly priced. In all cases, real estate is a poor tax shelter because the tax write-offs currently available are poor: 27.5 years for residential property and 31.5 years for commercial property. Investors buy real estate under various structures, and it is worthwhile to consider a few of the more popular ones.

    a) <u>Your own home</u>. This is often the best investment individuals can make.

    b) <u>Vacation properties</u> generally lose money. There is an abundance of vacation properties for sale and this drives down rental rates and selling prices. One difficulty is the risk of vacancy during the off-season. At best, most investors break even on the cash flow and have a nice place to visit.

    c) <u>Real Estate Investment Trusts (REITs)</u>. Investors buy shares in REITs which buy properties. Some REITs have been profitable, and others have gone bankrupt. Profitability depends on the properties the fund purchases, the success and skills of the management company, and the fees the management company and sponsor charges. Further, individual investors have no control over the real estate. REITs are generally a poor investment.

d) Time Shares represent ownership in a piece of real estate for a certain time period each year. For example, my neighbor owns a condominium in Puerto Rico during the first two weeks of November. Every year, he can stay in his condominium for those two weeks; rent out the condo; or trade his two weeks for two weeks in a condominium in a different location.

Some people like time shares because they represent ownership in real estate and the interest on the mortgage is currently tax deductible. The drawback is time shares are difficult to sell. If you want to own a vacation home, consider pooling your resources with your family to buy a property (note that I have seen families squabble over who should use the condo during say, Christmas - so you may be better off renting different vacation properties on your own).

e) Individual properties located in your neighborhood are often the best real estate investments individual investors can make. Often, two-family houses can be a good investment. Since you live in the town, you should understand the market, the prices, the trends, and the nature and quality of a property compared with other local properties. You will also be able to actively manage and monitor the property. On the other hand, investment properties can be burdensome to manage because you (unless you hire a property manager) must monitor the property, handle repairs, collect the rent, pay the mortgage, and find suitable tenants. Before investing, learn the real estate business; consider enrolling in a real estate investment course at a local business school or college.

**Mutual Funds**

*WHY SHOULD MOST INDIVIDUALS INVEST IN MUTUAL FUNDS?*

1. Most individual investors do not have the time to follow the market.

2. The majority of individual investors do not have the acumen to beat the stock market consistently.

3. Mutual funds enable individual investors to take advantage of economies of scale by pooling their money with other investors' money (this lowers transaction costs and enables individuals to benefit from the mutual fund's extensive research staff).

4. Mutual funds employ professional money managers who have the skills to invest money successfully.

A few thoughts on investing in mutual funds:

1. Invest in funds that meet your financial goals.

2. Choose funds comprised of investments you understand and like.

3. Choose well-managed funds sponsored by companies who have a solid reputation.

4. Invest for the long run. Don't continually switch investments. If you need money in the short run (less than five years), you should invest your money in a high quality money market mutual fund or a treasury bill mutual fund because the likelihood of earning a rate of return is higher.

5. Read the fund's prospectus before investing. Each mutual fund is chartered to invest in certain types of securities; see if a fund's objectives match yours. And, review the roster of investments (even though the investments may change over time) to assess the prospects for the fund.

6. Buy mutual funds directly. Stock brokers will gladly buy any mutual fund for you because they earn a commission which is over and above the mutual fund's fees.

7. "No-Load" funds. These funds charge ongoing management fees but do not charge commissions to buy and sell shares. There is no proof that the results differ significantly from "Load" funds. See Rules of Investing, #18.

8. Invest money every month in your mutual fund as described in Wealth - Building Strategies, #9. When the price of your mutual fund shares rises or falls, you take advantage of this by averaging the cost of your purchases (dollar cost averaging) since you invest the same amount of money every month. Over time, you should do well.

9. Study Forbes magazine's annual mutual fund guide (issued in late August or early September) which analyzes the performance of hundreds of mutual funds. Choose a few funds that meet your objectives, but research the fund before investing. Mutual fund offerings worthy of consideration include money market funds, common stock funds (equities), taxable and tax-exempt (state and municipal government) bond funds, US Government Treasury Bill funds, and GNMA's. Funds comprised of commodities, options and futures are usually losers. The table on the next page lists several mutual funds described in the Forbes magazine September 2, 1991 issue.

The following funds do not represent investment recommendations but merely ideas for further research:

| Mutual Fund Candidate | Type of Investment | Load/ No-Load | Phone Number |
|---|---|---|---|
| Dreyfus 100% US Treasury Money Market Fund | US Treasuries | No | 1-800-645-6561<br>1-800-782-6620 |
| Fidelity Blue Chip Growth Fund | C/S + | Yes | 1-800-544-8888 |
| Fidelity Magellan Fund | C/S | Yes | 1-800-544-8888 |
| Twentieth Century Growth | C/S | No | 1-800-345-2021 |
| Twentieth Century Select | C/S | No | 1-800-345-2021 |
| Vanguard Fixed Income US Treasuries | US Treasuries | No | 1-800-662-7447<br>1-215-648-6000 |
| Vanguard Fixed Income Fund | Bonds | No | 1-800-662-7447 |
| Vanguard GNMA Fund | GNMA | No | 1-800-662-7447 |
| Vanguard Index 500 Fund * | C/S | No | 1-800-662-7447 |

\+ C/S signifies common stock fund.

* The Vanguard Index 500 fund invests in the S&P (Standard & Poor's) 500 industrial stocks, and the fund trades securities only when the relative percentage of a common stock in the index changes. The ongoing expenses are low compared with other funds.

Many fund sponsors manage mutual funds comprised of common stocks in a specific industry group. Fidelity, for example, offers funds in energy, health care, biotechnology, and several other industries. If you want to concentrate on a specific industry, seek out these types of funds.

Many mutual fund companies offer funds which invest in securities which are exempt from Federal, state and local income taxes. Dreyfus and Fidelity offer these types of funds.

> Note: Past performance is not a good indicator of future performance although outstanding fund managers should on average produce good profits.

10. Invest some of your money in a high quality common stock mutual fund. In the short run, diversified common stock mutual funds may decline in value in the short run, but over the long run, many common stock mutual funds have earned excellent rates of return.

11. Diversify your investments (invest in different products). Some investments increase in value while other investments decline in value. By buying a mix of investment products, you can diversify your holdings and hopefully smooth out your returns on investment.

Note: As you accumulate wealth, make sure you have a proper will drafted by an attorney specializing in trusts and estates to protect your assets.

## *SIGNS OF TROUBLE*

Many people overlook this section of the guide because they don't want to admit they are a high-risk candidate for financial trouble. Okay, you don't have to tell anyone if you have these symptoms. But if you do have any of these symptoms, review your spending habits and Worksheet III.

Always run to the bank to withdraw money
Borrow from one credit card to pay down another
Depleting savings accounts
Drawing down lines of credit to live
Drink alcoholic beverages several times per week
Excessive credit card debt
Gambling (high stakes and often)
Home equity loans (excessive and frequent draw-downs)
Late on monthly payments
Negative balance in your checking account
Never pay full balance on credit card bill
Never have cash in your pocket
Pledging belongings at pawn shop
Second mortgage on house/condo for living expenses
Selling belongings often to raise money
Zero balance in your checking account

If any of these symptoms pertain to you, make sure you are taking every precaution to live within your means, and limit the amount of money available for discretionary items. It may be especially important for you to pay your bills automatically. Visit your banker and set up monthly wire transfers to move money from your checking account to your utility, telephone company, landlord, or credit card companies.

Although it may be difficult, be honest with yourself. If any of these signs pertain to you, reread this guide and be sure to follow every step to gain control over your finances.

## *82 STRATEGIES TO SAVE MONEY*

Sometimes, saving money is as simple as asking for a better deal, and other times, saving money entails planning and effort. These strategies are designed to make you feel more in control of yourself and your money. Many of these strategies improve health, help the environment, and save time, in addition to saving money. If you have any money-saving ideas, please send them to me, and I will try to include them in the next printing of this guide (any ideas submitted become the property of Career Advancement Center).

**Entertainment:**

1. Buy the current Entertainment, a coupon book. Entertainment Publishing offers this annual coupon book in approximately 130 cities in the United States. This book contains discount coupons for vacations, restaurants, and movie theaters. Participating hotels offer 50% discounts off their room-rates, and restaurants offer buy one entree, get one free. You can obtain information about the books available in your area by writing to: Entertainment Publications, Inc, Post Office Box 1909, Ann Arbor, Michigan 48106-1909. The book costs approximately $30, and if use the book, you'll recover the price of the book very quickly.

2. Buy the Transmedia Card. This is a dining card which entitles the holder to 20% - 25% discount off the cost of meals in selected restaurants. The annual fee is $50, but if you dine in restaurants often, you'll save many dollars. Call Transmedia at 1-800-422-5090 or write: Transmedia Network Inc., 1900 Biscayne Blvd., North Miami, Florida 33181.

3. Seek out bargain-priced or free events. In New York City, the museums offer free admission on Tuesdays. Many people attend Shakespeare in the Park (Central Park). The City sponsors outdoor concerts in various parks which are also free of charge. Chicago City Limits, a comedy improvisation group in New York City, performs several nights each week; the ticket price is very reasonable, and the show is outstanding.

   Many restaurants offer dinner specials for eating before a certain hour (perhaps 6PM), and on certain evenings (Monday or Tuesday), the restaurant may offer free dessert or drinks.

4. Host a Movie Night. When I was in accounting, eleven of my peers worked on one audit, and once a month, someone would host a movie night. Everyone brought something to eat or drink, and we rented a movie from the local video store. This was an inexpensive way to have fun.

5. Enroll in a class. The YMCA for example, offers courses on topics from folklore to photography. The cost is reasonable and it's lots of fun. Chicago City Limits, the New York City based comedy improvisation group also offers comedy classes. Many adult education programs and churches offer classes.

6. Eat home or bring your lunch to work. Buy a thermos; soda and packaged drinks are usually expensive. Drink water. Also, buy packages of snacks in the supermarket at reduced prices and store them in the office. Bring fruit or granola bars from home and avoid the vending machines. Better yet, avoid extra calories by not eating between meals.

   Aside from perhaps pizza, eating in restaurants generally costs substantially more than a home-cooked meal. And, save the leftovers for another meal.

7. Subscribe to your favorite magazines. A one-year subscription costs about half the newsstand price. Besides, a magazine will be a welcome relief from the junk mail.

**Shopping:**

8. Buy the house brands. Today, supermarkets are investing money in their house brands because the store earns higher profits than on the name brands. The higher investment translates into superior product quality, and you may save 20%-30% by buying the house brands.

9. Use store coupons to buy cosmetics, drug items, and groceries. You can cut coupons from the newspapers or receive them in the mail, and if you make the effort, you should save at least $100 per year. And, take advantage of product-rebate offers.

10. Don't spend money. If you postpone or cancel a purchase, you automatically save money. For every dollar of salary you earn, you must pay income taxes to the government; therefore, at the 30% tax rate, for every dollar you earn, like Jack, you take home only $0.70. Therefore, saving one dollar is equivalent to earning a pre-tax salary of approximately $1.43 ($1.00 divided by 0.70) but requires less effort.

11. Delay your major purchases. Salespeople urge you to purchase today because they claim the sale price will be effective only for a limited time or the product will be out of stock permanently. So what!!! If the product is such a hot product, the store will order more from the manufacturer, and if the current model is hot, the manufacturer will sell a new and improved model next year. This year's model becomes last year's model and should be cheaper.

12. Don't buy impulsively. Once in a while, look around your house and notice all the things you "had to have." If you are like me, you probably haven't used many of those things in years. You could probably safely get by without 25% of the things you own. And that would add up to a significant amount of money. Think: do you have this or a similar item already? Do you really need this item?

13. Sell the items you never use. Periodically, sell items you bought on a whim and haven't used for at least one year. Many people have garage sales.

14. Repair your things instead of buying new ones. Many people have little patience for tinkering with the toolbox. Or, get your things repaired; it is less expensive to have your shoes repaired than buying a new pair. If you take a few minutes, you may find that repairing household items is satisfying, easy and can save hundreds of dollars.

15. Buy on sale. If you studied Economics 101, you are familiar with the laws of supply and demand. When demand is low and supply is high, the price of a product falls. If times are bad, sales are probably low, and shopkeepers welcome business, and you should get your biggest discount. The bigger the inventory, the more eager the merchant is to sell. Don't forget to negotiate for better prices and terms. Also, shop around before buying.

16. Join a shopping warehouse. The service is minimal, but the prices are the lowest around. Several stores are Costco, Sam's Wholesale Clubs, and Price Company.

17. Buy quality. My Dad continually reminds me that buying the best product in its class, even if it costs more today, will pay for itself over the long run. Many people buy the least expensive item in the store and find that they buy the same item every year when last year's model breaks. Conduct your research and pay a little extra today, and you should minimize your long term costs.

18. Use the Public Library. One of my hobbies is reading, and during my peak reading season, I read about one book every week. For some crazy reason, I feel compelled to buy the books even though I give away most of the books when I finish reading them. My colleagues and I have set up a book barter program at work, but my bank account balance would be higher if I visited the Public Library.

19. Quit smoking and start exercising. If you quit smoking, you'll save about $2.25 per pack of cigarettes, and your doctor's bills should decline. One stubborn smoker told me he continues to smoke so he won't live long enough to deplete his wealth; interesting logic.

    If you stop smoking and exercise, you should feel better and require less medical care, but start a program only with the advice of your doctor.

20. Become a comparative shopper. You should have tremendous bargaining power and save a lot of money if you develop an understanding of the prices of goods. Before making major purchases, follow newspaper ads for a few weeks and purchase a copy of Consumer's Reports to learn about various products and features. Visit several stores and negotiate the best deal.

21. Change your wardrobe inexpensively. With clothes, you probably have old outfits which you rarely or never wear; wear them. Also, create new outfits by mixing and matching pieces of your current wardrobe. Simple additions such as a new belt, tie, or earrings can result in a new outfit which costs significantly less than a new outfit. Of course, you could trade your clothes; my brother and I swap ties.

**Your Credit Cards:**

22. Cancel some of your credit cards. Many people have several credit cards which charge annual fees of $20. They probably don't need all the credit cards they have because most credit cards are accepted universally. Dump the ones that overlap, and request higher credit lines if necessary.

23. Switch to credit cards which charge no annual membership fee and you will save $20 per card on average. Two cards with no annual membership fees are: ATT Universal Card (1-800-CALL-ATT) (although ATT is considering charging a fee) and Sears Discover Card (1-800-347-2683). Consider dropping the more expensive cards such as American Express which charges $55 per year for the green card and $75 for the gold card.

24. Switch to a credit card which charges lower interest rates. People who carry large balances on their credit cards probably pay interest at rates between 19% and 21% per year. Using credit cards which charge a lower interest rate should result in big savings.

25. Lock your credit cards in a drawer. If you tend to use your credit cards for everything and carry large outstanding balances, consider canceling all your credit cards or locking them in a drawer. This should prevent you from running up big balances and incurring interest charges. If you have gotten into trouble with your credit cards before, you are at increased risk; monitor your charge habits closely.

26. Use credit cards after the billing cycle ends. Suppose your Visa cycle runs from January 16 through February 15. This means that every charge you make between those dates should appear on your February 15 statement, and the payment should be due on March 15. If you defer your purchase until February 17, the charge should miss the February 15 statement and appear on your March 15 bill; the payment should be due on April 15. You have your purchase and have deferred payment and most likely avoided interest charges for about six weeks.

27. Always pay off your credit card in full. Your monthly credit card statement shows the total amount due and also the minimum payment required. Last month, my Visa bill was $600 and the minimum amount due was $20. If banks make it so easy for you to borrow their money, consumers must be getting a bad deal: banks charge interest at 20% per year on the outstanding balance.

    If you pay the minimum amount due on your credit card for several consecutive months, your balance increases geometrically. Suppose your total bill is $1,000; the minimum payment due might equal $40. Your credit card company charges 20% interest on the outstanding balance of $960 (if you pay the $40 minimum), and your annual interest bill might equal $210. You could buy some nice things with $210.

**Travelling:**

28. Enroll in frequent flyer programs. Most airlines, hotels, and rent-a-car companies sponsor bonus programs where they award frequent travellers miles and points towards future hotel stays and airline tickets. Many airlines award free tickets after you accumulate 20,000 miles. Usually, there is no cost to join.

    To help you accumulate miles, some banks have jumped into the frequent traveller program. For example, Citibank's American Advantage Visa card (1-800-843-0777) awards one mile on your American Airlines frequent flyer account for every dollar you charge on your Visa card. First Chicago's Mileage Plus card (1-800-368-4535) awards miles towards United Airlines. The annual fees range from $50 to $100, and while I certainly do not advocate using your credit cards just for the sake of accumulating frequent flyer miles, if you charge enough, this can be a worthwhile way to get free travel.

29. Carpool to work. Your neighbors may work downtown. If three people share the driving, the commuting cost drops 66%. Make sure you enjoy the people you share your trip with. Also, leaving your car at home should reduce the wear and tear and maintenance costs; and extend your car's life.

30. Walk, or bike to work. Despite the cost savings, you will relax and get exercise.

**Your Car:**

31. Reduce your driving. If you own a car, use the car less frequently, or do all your driving during one trip. For example, if you have five errands to run, combine them to save gas, wear and tear on the car, and time.

32. Buy a new car. If your car is beyond repair, it may pay to buy a new one although this may affect your loan and insurance payments (Worksheet III, line 5). Yes, in certain circumstances you can save money by buying a new car.

Upon concluding that you need to own a car, figure out how much money you spend annually to maintain the car. In addition to routine check-ups, the older your car, the more costly it is to maintain. After a car hits 50,000 miles, you may need a new transmission and brakes. These items can be worthwhile investments provided you expect your car to last another 30,000 miles without additional major problems. New cars should require less maintenance. Larger cars typically consume more gasoline which can be a factor in determining whether to buy a more fuel efficient car. If you currently own a sports car and your new car is outside the sports car category, your insurance costs should decline. In these cases, buying a new car may save you money.

33. Do your own repairs. There are many car repair books on the market which explain basic repairs.

34. Service Station Repairs. If you need to have repairs done at a service station, be sure to get a price quote before the mechanic does any work. Also, instruct the repairman not to perform any additional work without your permission and a price quote or firm estimate (range of costs).

35. Premium gas. Don't buy premium or super gas unless your car manual recommends it. And, pump your own gas (self-service); you'll save approximately $0.25 per gallon.

36. Service your car every 3,000 miles. The best way to extend the life of your car is to change the oil and get a tune-up every 3,000 miles. And, every 15,000 miles, change the transmission oil. Your car should run better and the mechanic should locate any emerging problems. Performing preventive maintenance should reduce your major repair costs over the life of the car as well as extend the life of your car.

37. Don't buy a car. In Strategy #32, I recommend buying a new car, but in this strategy, I want to point out that buying a car is very costly. Cars are wasting assets (they generally lose one-third of their value upon leaving the dealership). First, there is the cost of the car. Second, there are the interest and principal payments on the car loan. If you buy a new car and you borrow money, factor the loan payments into your budget. Also, any cash you spend to buy the car or make a down payment is gone: you cannot invest the cash to earn interest and build wealth. Third, there are insurance, parking and maintenance costs. All in all, owning a car is a losing proposition.

If you live in a city which has an extensive public transit system, travel via bus, train, or taxi is easy. And when you want to travel long distances, renting a car during numerous weekends may still result in tremendous savings over owning a car.

38. Sell your car. If you are married or live with your parents, maybe you don't need a car. If you own two cars, maybe you could survive with only one. Some people have two cars but store one in a garage; they save insurance and maintenance.

**Insurance:**

39. Compare insurance plans and companies. Buy insurance from a credit-worthy company who has a record of paying claims (ask your insurance broker or librarian for the A.M. Best rating which rates the financial strength of the insurer). Different companies offer insurance plans which provide different levels of coverage at different prices. Conduct careful research.

40. Consider increasing your deductible. The deductible is the amount of money you will pay in the event of a casualty. Often this amount is $250, $500, or $1,000. If your deductible is $500, in the event of a loss, you will pay the first $500 and the insurance company should pay you for covered items lost in excess of $500 up to the face value of your policy or the loss (whichever is lower). The higher your deductible, the lower your insurance premiums and the more you pay in the event of a loss. Evaluate the likelihood of a loss and the premium savings in relation to the extra money you would lose by having a higher deductible in the event of loss.

41. Take a safe driving course. The National Safety Council (1-800-962-3434) offers defensive driving courses. Graduates can take advantage of reduced car insurance premiums or reduced points on their driver's license. The one-day course runs for four - five hours. The course costs approximately $50 and the insurance discount can total $300 over a three year period. In addition, you may learn something which could save your life.

42. Cancel insurance policies which provide duplicate coverage. Sometimes, people carry two policies which insure the same asset, and the insurance company will pay for the loss only once; therefore, premiums paid are wasted. Sometimes you can get a refund for duplicate premiums paid.

**Your Vacations:**

43. Take your vacation off-season. During the peak season, people flock to the vacation spots, and the hotel rates are top dollar. During the slower seasons, hotel vacancy rises and the room-rates drop. Some individuals own condominiums for investment purposes and often the vacancy rates are high; since the owners make mortgage and maintenance payments all year-round regardless of the occupancy, they want to rent out their condo. Search for bargains and make a deal.

44. Research less popular vacation spots. The cost is less and the spot is less crowded, but the vacation can be just as nice and perhaps more interesting than the usual spot. Remember too, that if the local economy relies on tourism for a large percentage of its income, the service should be better because they want you to recommend the site to your friends.

45. Analyze the tour/package prices. Often, vacation packages which include hotel, airfare, and meals are more costly than if you book the trip yourself. This difference represents the tour packager's profit. Remember that the tour leader books numerous rooms and flights and already receives a discount which they may or may not share with you.

46. Vacation with your car instead of an airplane. If you already own a car or can borrow one, you can eliminate the cost of airfare. An automobile trip may not be as exotic as a plane trip to a faraway island, but the cost is not out of this world either.

47. Defer your vacation for six months. Many people pay for their vacations with credit cards. Unfortunately, they don't have the money in their bank account to pay the credit card bill when its due, and they build up loan balances which accrue interest at about 20% per year. In effect, they pay for their vacation twice: once for the cost of the trip and once through the cost of the credit card interest.

    The best plan is to save money every month in a separate savings account to ensure you will have enough money to pay for the entire vacation when the credit card bill arrives (see section Other Budgeting Tips).

48. Spend your next vacation at home. If you don't have the money to take an exotic trip, don't worry. There must be plenty of fun things to do which are in your city or a short car-ride away. Any change of pace should help your psyche. Don't feel compelled to pile on the credit card debt to take an exotic trip.

49. Tie your vacation to a business trip. This is an old favorite. Suppose your company sends you to a trade show in California and the company pays your airfare. When the conference is done, plan to stay an extra week to experience the beaches. Most likely, you will pay only the incremental hotel and the site-seeing costs.

50. Get the Continental Airlines Freedom Passport. Continental offers a great travel program for people aged 62 and older. With some restrictions, you can make one, one-way trip in the continental US every week for the entire year. The Freedom Passport costs $1,799. Call Continental at 1-800-441-1135.

51. Buy the Entertainment book for your destination city (see strategy #1). My friend Howard planned a trip to Hawaii. The Hawaii book contained a coupon for a buy-one, get-one helicopter ride free worth $130. Howard and his wife saved $130. They also took advantage of the discounts on meals and lodging.

    Many hotels offer AAA (Automobile Association of America) and AARP (American Association of Retired Persons) members a 5%-10% discount off the regular room-rates. This is free money; just remember to carry you membership card in your wallet or suitcase.

52. Compare prices. Different travel agents sometimes quote different prices for the same trip. Also, leaving at a different time, leaving on a different day, or staying at your destination over a Saturday night can result in lower airfares and hotel rates. At times, it can be advantageous to book your trip 30 days before departure.

**Your Taxes:**

53. Hire a good accountant (CPA) to prepare your taxes. A good CPA should help reduce your tax bill by applying the tax law to your specific circumstances. Ask your friends if they would recommend their CPA. If you hire a CPA, get several references and speak with some of his clients.

54. Maintain organized records of your checking account activity and spending habits, and set up an annual receipts file. You should save tax dollars because you can review your financial history easily and recall deductible items. The worst strategy is to meet your accountant on April 14, with a shopping bag full of receipts in hand because you will spend more time sorting the papers than taking advantage of deductions. Inevitably, you will miss deductions and pay more tax than necessary.

55. Make your estimated tax payments as close to the deadline as possible and keep the money in a special savings account to earn interest income. Receiving a tax refund from the government is great, except this means the government has free use of your money. Your accountant should calculate your minimum estimated quarterly payments to avoid a penalty. Suppose you have to make four estimated payments of $300 or $1,200 in total. If you divide the total tax bill by 12 and deposit $100 in a money market mutual fund or savings account every month, you should earn interest income and can send the money to Uncle Sam when its due.

56. Save your tax refunds. Sound money management entails spending at most your take-home salary. If you receive a tax refund, save it; it should not be money you counted on so deposit the money in your savings account immediately, and let it grow.

57. Minimize your tax refunds by paying less taxes during the year. If you receive a large refund every year ($1,000 or more), you are wasting money because the government has free use of your money. Your accountant may suggest you reduce your tax withholdings. Raising the number of exemptions you take should increase your take-home pay, but be sure to invest the money.

58. Move to a city or state with lower tax rates. Currently, several states do not levy state income taxes; two are Florida and Texas. It is possible to move several miles from your old town to a lower tax jurisdiction. But research sales and use taxes, and property taxes. Consider the increased commuting time if you retain your current job or the cost of housing in the new neighborhood. Also, employers in the new area may pay lower salaries and this may result in little or no incremental savings.

59. Open an IRA (individual retirement account) or 401K plan. These plans allow individuals to save money for retirement tax-free. One's taxable income is reduced by the amount of the contributions. For example, if you earn $25,000 per year and deposit $2,000 in your IRA account, Uncle Sam taxes you on $23,000. The interest accumulates tax-free although you will pay taxes on your withdrawals. There are restrictions and penalties under certain circumstances associated with withdrawals and limits on the deductibility of your contribution if your income exceeds a certain amount, so consult a CPA. This can be an excellent way to save money for retirement.

60. Pay any state income taxes due before December 31 if you itemize your Federal Income Tax Return. Under current Federal Tax Law, taxpayers who itemize their tax deductions can deduct the state income tax they paid during the tax year from their Federal income. For example, if Jack pays state income taxes equal to $2,200 in 1992 and he itemizes his Federal Income Tax Return, Jack can deduct the $2,200 in state income taxes from his Federal Income. Preparing tax returns is complex, so consult a reputable CPA.

61. Donate old clothing and other items to goodwill. If you itemize your Federal Income Tax Return, this strategy should increase your charitable contributions and your tax deductions. Be sure to obtain a valid receipt. Preparing tax returns is complex, so consult a reputable CPA.

62. Pay taxes on time to avoid penalties and interest charges. Why pay the government more money than you have to?

**Your Finances:**

63. Barter. Most of us accumulate junk over time, and it may be that the things (clothes, furniture, books and countless other items) that conquer our closets have little value to us but may be valuable to someone else. Trade these items for goods or services you want. You should save plenty of money.

64. Create a rolling budget. Suppose your budget allows you to spend $100 every week. On Sunday night, you find $20 in your wallet. Excellent; you spent only $80 last week. You could give yourself a bonus and spend that $20 plus the $100 budget next week. Or, you could withdraw only $80 for the next week and use the extra $20 from last week to total your $100 weekly budget. Roll forward the $20 left over from last week into next week's budget, and deposit the extra $20 in your savings account to earn interest.

65. Live within your budget. You have set a budget for a reason, and if your budget is reasonable, you should be able to live within it. And, don't deviate. Many people establish a budget and don't follow it: they set out to spend $100 every week but withdraw cash from their checking account whenever they need money. It is impossible to monitor how much money one spends this way.

66. Save bonuses and overtime money in your special savings account. When I was in public accounting, my firm paid me overtime plus a $15 dinner allowance when I worked late. I saved all the overtime money I earned plus half the dinner allowances and expense reimbursements. This was a great way to build wealth.

67. Tax-free Bond Funds. Many mutual fund companies offer tax-free bond funds. Investing in bonds is very complex and outside the scope of this guide; nonetheless, under certain circumstances with the proper understanding and advice, it can be beneficial to buy these securities which can be exempt from federal, state, and local income taxes.

68. Save your loose change. Wrap the coins, and deposit them in your special bank account. I recently rolled $25 in coins I accumulated in a jar. It felt like found money.

69. Debt consolidation loans. Sometimes credit card debts become burdensome, and a debt consolidation loan converts onerous credit card debt into a single term loan which should bear a lower interest rate. Remember, the key to a debt consolidation loan is to pay off debt, not free up your credit lines to borrow more money. Once you decide to reduce your debt, don't go haywire with the charge cards.

70. Review your expenses and cut the unnecessary ones. The most effective way to do this is to review your check book (see section: Your Checkbook). Figure out your spending habits and then determine which expenditures you could defer, reduce, or eliminate. If you typically spend $40 on new clothes every month, you could cut your expenses in half by buying $40 of clothes every other month.

71. Save unusual cash items in your special savings account. Unusual items could include income tax refunds, product rebates, gifts, inheritances, lottery winnings, salary from second job or special projects, and an annual bonus. If you spend your base salary and save these extras, you should accumulate wealth at a surprisingly fast rate.

72. Get a second part-time job and save your whole salary. Many secretaries do part-time typing for other companies over the weekend or in the evenings. If possible, consider one of the tougher and more lucrative jobs: tending bar or waiting tables. Save the salary from your second job and you should build a nice savings account. Also see the ideas for starting your own business (see strategy #82).

73. Make extra payments on your mortgage or loans. Payments in excess of the contractual amount reduce the principal which in turn lowers your interest expense (see the section Borrowing Money). Banks charge interest on the outstanding loan balance, and the lower the outstanding balance, the lower the interest expense. Keep in mind that extra payments will not reduce your obligation to pay any future monthly payments.

74. Avoid taking out home equity loans. Some people take out so-called home equity loans to obtain more cash. Today, banks are heavily marketing these loans, but remember, heavily advertised deals generally benefit the banks more than you.

    Here's an example. Suppose your house is worth $100,000 and when you bought it, you borrowed $75,000 in the form of a mortgage. In effect, the bank owns the first $75,000 of the house if you default on the loan, and you own the remaining $25,000. The $25,000 portion is your equity. Under a home equity loan, banks lend money against your equity in the house, maybe up to $25,000 in this case.

    Don't forget that the bank "owns" your house until you pay off your mortgage. The bank holds your house as security (collateral) for the original mortgage plus the amount of the home equity loan.

Home equity loans are often a desperate attempt to raise money and are best avoided if possible. Although there can be valid reasons to borrow more money against the value of your house (including debt consolidation or converting non-tax-deductible interest expense into tax-deductible interest expense - consult a CPA before taking out such a loan), remember you must make additional payments to service the loan and this reduces the amount of money you can spend on other items. And, if you fail to repay the loan, you risk losing your house to the bank.

75. Examine and dispute incorrect bills. I always add up the items that appear on my restaurant checks and eyeball the sales tax; it is incredible how often my neighbor's drink appears on my bill. And, even computers make mistakes sometimes. In addition, a company who makes an error in your bill, may adjust your bill quickly, to maintain your loyalty.

**Your Home:**

76. Negotiate for a reduction in your rent expense. If you are a good tenant (quiet, pay your rent on time, haven't damaged your apartment), your landlord may prefer to keep you as a tenant as opposed to risk a vacant apartment and losing rental income. First, secure a renewal option, and then, ask for a rent reduction, zero rent increase, or at least a new paint job.

77. Get a roommate. Very often, two people can live together less expensively than two people living alone. Some people rent a one-bedroom apartment and divide the living room into two rooms. One half the room remains the living room and the second half becomes the second bedroom. It may be possible to cut your rent bill in half. Or, if the cash really gets tight, you could move in with relatives.

78. Cut your home energy costs. Many houses and apartments are poorly insulated and waste energy. By making a few simple additions such as insulation, and window and door guards, you can reduce your energy bills. Many utilities publish guides on how to cut home energy costs. Another source of energy-saving products is The Energy Store (located in California); contact them at 1-800-288-1938.

79. Cut your telephone bill. The easiest way to reduce your payments to Ma Bell is to stay off the phone. Most people don't write letters, so it pays to manage the telephone bills. Call your local phone company to find out when the discount calling periods are. Generally they are all day Saturday, Sundays until 5PM and weekdays after 6PM plus an additional discount after 11PM or midnight. Also, look up phone numbers in the phone book instead of calling directory assistance at $0.55 per call. Contact long distance services such as ATT (1-800-CALL-ATT), MCI (1-800-444-4444), Metromedia (formerly ITT) (1-800-275-0200), and Sprint (1-800-877-4646) to find the lowest rates for the areas you typically call. MCI has a program called

"Friends and Family" where you can select several frequently called telephone numbers and whenever you call those numbers, you receive a 20% discount off the regular rates (although both parties must use MCI as their primary long distance carrier).

80. Turn out the lights and turn down the thermostat. You will save money if you turn out the lights when you leave a room or leave the house. Buy energy-saving light bulbs. In the winter, turn down the thermostat so your heater doesn't work so hard, and wear a sweater.

81. Buy used furniture, and refinish it. It is easy to repaint furniture. It may turn your stomach to consider buying used furniture, and that is understandable, but consider this idea as a way to spur your creativity to save money. College students and young medical doctors are transient; they tend to move frequently. If you visit these neighborhoods, many tenants post signs in their lobby or laundry room offering furniture and stereos for sale: "Moving - must sell..." The prices are usually excellent although the quality may be questionable. You have nothing to lose by looking.

**Your Own Business:**

82. Start your own business (develop a second source of income). It's probably a safe bet that many readers would shake with fear if they actually considered starting their own business, and that's very understandable. First, starting a business does not mean you have to quit your job. Second, starting a business does not mean you have to invest six times your life savings or a lot of money. Third, if you choose to start your own venture, consult others who have done so and hire a reputable lawyer and CPA; you should avoid many pitfalls over the long run.

    The most successful businesses fill customers' needs. Look around you: could you provide a valuable service which people would pay for? What expertise do you have which others would buy? Start-up costs for certain service businesses may be merely the cost of printing flyers for advertising, printing business cards, or sending letters to prospective customers. Consider these simple businesses:

    1) Baby-sitting/Baby-sitting Service.
    2) Companion for the Elderly.
    3) Errand/Messenger Service (walk dogs; buy groceries).
    4) Computer Graphics and Word Processing (if you have a computer).
    5) House-cleaning Service.
    6) Catering Service.
    7) Real Estate (property) Management Service.

## *CONCLUSION*

This is the end of the written text, but hopefully the beginning of a new thought process for managing your money.

And, just because you may be about to close the book, don't forget all the great work you have done and all the concepts and strategies you have learned. The key is to put these thoughts and processes to work for you.

From time to time, pull the guide off the shelf, and compare your progress to your original plan. Use the strategies as a refresher course to keep your money-management skills sharp.

Hopefully, you completed all the worksheets. Review the financial goals you set and your net worth. Then, tie your goals and net worth to your financial budget and work to achieve your goals. If you have set a budget, stick to it, and implement the strategies to save money. You should accumulate wealth easily and quickly.

Best wishes for financial success. And, let me know your thoughts and ideas.

Eric Gelb
c/o Career Advancement Center, Inc.
Post Office Box 436
Woodmere, New York 11598-0436

# WORKSHEET I

## Statement of Financial Goals

| OBJECTIVE: | Year | Final Amount | Monthly Deposit |
|---|---|---|---|
| Example: Buy a Condominium | 1995 | $7,200 | $136.08 |
| Example: Buy a Condominium | 1995 | $6,565 | $124.08 |
| | | | |
| | | | |
| | | | |
| | | | |
| | | | |
| | | | |
| | | | |
| | | | |
| | | | |
| | | | |
| | | | |
| | | | |
| | | | |
| | | | |
| | | | |
| | | | |
| | | | |
| | | | |
| | | | |

# WORKSHEET II

YEAR: ____________

## STATEMENT of NET WORTH

| ASSETS: | Total Amount | Interest Rate | Monthly Payment / Income |
|---|---|---|---|
| Savings Accounts: | | | |
| | | | |
| | | | |
| Mutual Funds: | | | |
| | | | |
| Personal Residence: | | | |
| | | | |
| TOTAL ASSETS: | | | |
| LIABILITIES: | | | |
| Credit Card Debt: | | | |
| Visa / Mastercard: | | | |
| Visa / Mastercard: | | | |
| Other: | | | |
| | | | |
| Car Loans: | | | |
| | | | |
| Student Loans: | | | |
| Mortgage: | | | |
| Taxes: | | | |
| TOTAL LIABILITIES: | | | |
| NET WORTH: | | | |

## WORKSHEET II

YEAR: ____________

## STATEMENT of NET WORTH

| ASSETS: | Total Amount | Interest Rate | Monthly Payment / Income |
|---|---|---|---|
| Savings Accounts: | | | |
| | | | |
| | | | |
| | | | |
| Mutual Funds: | | | |
| | | | |
| | | | |
| Personal Residence: | | | |
| | | | |
| | | | |
| TOTAL ASSETS: | | | |
| LIABILITIES: | | | |
| Credit Card Debt: | | | |
| Visa / Mastercard: | | | |
| Visa / Mastercard: | | | |
| Other: | | | |
| | | | |
| Car Loans: | | | |
| | | | |
| | | | |
| Student Loans: | | | |
| | | | |
| Mortgage: | | | |
| | | | |
| Taxes: | | | |
| TOTAL LIABILITIES: | | | |
| NET WORTH: | | | |

# WORKSHEET III

YEAR: ____________

## PERSONAL BUDGET PLANNER

| | | Yourself | Partner | Total |
|---|---|---|---|---|
| | **INCOME:** | | | |
| 1 | Salary before taxes: | | | |
| 2 | Total withholdings: | | | |
| 3 | Net income: | | | |
| | **FIXED EXPENSES:** | | | |
| 4 | Housing expenses: | | | |
| 5 | Loan payments: | | | |
| 6 | Insurance premiums: | | | |
| 7 | Total fixed expenses: | | | |
| | **PERIODIC COSTS:** | | | |
| 8 | Commuting cost: | | | |
| 9 | Personal beauty care: | | | |
| 10 | Medical costs: | | | |
| 11 | Car repair costs: | | | |
| 12 | Income tax payments: | | | |
| 13 | Total periodic costs: | | | |
| | **ONGOING OUT OF POCKET EXPENSES:** | | | |
| 14 | Cash spending budget: | | | |
| 15 | Credit card payments: | | | |
| 16 | Xmas, birthday, gifts: | | | |
| 17 | Telephone / utilities: | | | |
| 18 | Other expenses: | | | |
| 19 | Total out of pocket: | | | |
| 20 | Other income: | | | |
| 21 | Net surplus (deficit): | | | |
| 22 | Vacation allowance: | | | |
| 23 | Savings goal: | | | |
| 24 | Total surplus (deficit): | | | |

# WORKSHEET III

YEAR: ____________

# PERSONAL BUDGET PLANNER

| | | Yourself | Partner | Total |
|---|---|---|---|---|
| | **INCOME:** | | | |
| 1 | Salary before taxes: | | | |
| 2 | Total withholdings: | | | |
| 3 | Net income: | | | |
| | **FIXED EXPENSES:** | | | |
| 4 | Housing expenses: | | | |
| 5 | Loan payments: | | | |
| 6 | Insurance premiums: | | | |
| 7 | Total fixed expenses: | | | |
| | **PERIODIC COSTS:** | | | |
| 8 | Commuting cost: | | | |
| 9 | Personal beauty care: | | | |
| 10 | Medical costs: | | | |
| 11 | Car repair costs: | | | |
| 12 | Income tax payments: | | | |
| 13 | Total periodic costs: | | | |
| | **ONGOING OUT OF POCKET EXPENSES:** | | | |
| 14 | Cash spending budget: | | | |
| 15 | Credit card payments: | | | |
| 16 | Xmas, birthday, gifts: | | | |
| 17 | Telephone / utilities: | | | |
| 18 | Other expenses: | | | |
| 19 | Total out of pocket: | | | |
| 20 | Other income: | | | |
| 21 | Net surplus (deficit): | | | |
| 22 | Vacation allowance: | | | |
| 23 | Savings goal: | | | |
| 24 | Total surplus (deficit): | | | |

# WORKSHEET III

YEAR: ____________

# PERSONAL BUDGET PLANNER

| | | Yourself | Partner | Total |
|---|---|---|---|---|
| | **INCOME:** | | | |
| 1 | Salary before taxes: | | | |
| 2 | Total withholdings: | | | |
| 3 | Net income: | | | |
| | **FIXED EXPENSES:** | | | |
| 4 | Housing expenses: | | | |
| 5 | Loan payments: | | | |
| 6 | Insurance premiums: | | | |
| 7 | Total fixed expenses: | | | |
| | **PERIODIC COSTS:** | | | |
| 8 | Commuting cost: | | | |
| 9 | Personal beauty care: | | | |
| 10 | Medical costs: | | | |
| 11 | Car repair costs: | | | |
| 12 | Income tax payments: | | | |
| 13 | Total periodic costs: | | | |
| | **ONGOING OUT OF POCKET EXPENSES:** | | | |
| 14 | Cash spending budget: | | | |
| 15 | Credit card payments: | | | |
| 16 | Xmas, birthday, gifts: | | | |
| 17 | Telephone / utilities: | | | |
| 18 | Other expenses: | | | |
| 19 | Total out of pocket: | | | |
| 20 | Other income: | | | |
| 21 | Net surplus (deficit): | | | |
| 22 | Vacation allowance: | | | |
| 23 | Savings goal: | | | |
| 24 | Total surplus (deficit): | | | |

## WORKSHEET IV

## CALCULATING PRESENT VALUE
## USE WITH FINANCIAL TABLE I

| Years | Interest Rate | Factor From Fin'l. Table I | Final Amount | Present Value: Factor Multiplied by Final Amount |
|---|---|---|---|---|
| 4 | 7.00% | 0.7564 | $7,200.00 | $5,446.08 |
| 4 | 10.00% | 0.6715 | $7,200.00 | $4,834.80 |
| 4 | 7.00% | 0.7564 | $6,564.80 | $4,965.61 |
| | | | | |
| | | | | |
| | | | | |
| | | | | |
| | | | | |
| | | | | |
| | | | | |
| | | | | |
| | | | | |
| | | | | |
| | | | | |
| | | | | |
| | | | | |
| | | | | |
| | | | | |
| | | | | |
| | | | | |
| | | | | |
| | | | | |
| | | | | |
| | | | | |

# WORKSHEET V

## CALCULATING FUTURE VALUE
## USE WITH FINANCIAL TABLE II

| Years | Interest Rate | Factor From Fin'l. Table II | Present Value | Future Value: Factor Multiplied by Present Value |
|---|---|---|---|---|
| 4 | 6.00% | 1.2704 | $500.00 | $635.20 |
| | | | | |
| | | | | |
| | | | | |
| | | | | |
| | | | | |
| | | | | |
| | | | | |
| | | | | |
| | | | | |
| | | | | |
| | | | | |
| | | | | |
| | | | | |
| | | | | |
| | | | | |
| | | | | |
| | | | | |
| | | | | |
| | | | | |
| | | | | |
| | | | | |
| | | | | |

# WORKSHEET VI

## CALCULATING MONTHLY DEPOSITS (ANNUITIES) USE WITH FINANCIAL TABLE III

| Years | Interest Rate | Factor From Fin'l. Table III | Final Amount | Monthly Pmt.: Factor Multiplied by Final Amount |
|---|---|---|---|---|
| 4 | 5.00% | 0.0189 | $7,200.00 | $136.08 |
| 4 | 5.00% | 0.0189 | $6,565.00 | $124.08 |
| | | | | |
| | | | | |
| | | | | |
| | | | | |
| | | | | |
| | | | | |
| | | | | |
| | | | | |
| | | | | |
| | | | | |
| | | | | |
| | | | | |
| | | | | |
| | | | | |
| | | | | |
| | | | | |
| | | | | |
| | | | | |
| | | | | |
| | | | | |
| | | | | |
| | | | | |

# WORKSHEET VII

## CALCULATING FUTURE VALUE OF MONTHLY DEPOSITS (ANNUITIES) USE WITH FINANCIAL TABLE IV

| Years | Interest Rate | Factor From Fin'l. Table IV | Monthly Deposit | Future Value: Factor Multiplied by Monthly Deposit |
|---|---|---|---|---|
| 4 | 5.00% | 53.0148 | $75.00 | $3,976.11 |
| | | | | |
| | | | | |
| | | | | |
| | | | | |
| | | | | |
| | | | | |
| | | | | |
| | | | | |
| | | | | |
| | | | | |
| | | | | |
| | | | | |
| | | | | |
| | | | | |
| | | | | |
| | | | | |
| | | | | |
| | | | | |
| | | | | |
| | | | | |
| | | | | |
| | | | | |

# WORKSHEET VIII

## PRE – TAX VERSUS AFTER – TAX MONEY

This worksheet calculates pre – tax dollars needed to attain after –tax goals.

| Take – Home Pay per Pay Period [1] | Gross Salary Per Pay Period [2] | Ratio: [1] divided by [2] [3] | After – tax Financial Goal [4] | Pre – tax Goal [4] divided by [3] [5] | Salary Per Day or Per Week [6] | Minimum Days / Weeks of Work [5] divided by [6] [7] |
|---|---|---|---|---|---|---|
| $875.00 | $1,250.00 | 0.70 | $2,589.00 | $3,698.57 | $50.00 | 73.97 |
| | | | | | | |
| | | | | | | |
| | | | | | | |
| | | | | | | |
| | | | | | | |
| | | | | | | |
| | | | | | | |
| | | | | | | |
| | | | | | | |
| | | | | | | |
| | | | | | | |
| | | | | | | |
| | | | | | | |
| | | | | | | |
| | | | | | | |

# FINANCIAL TABLE I

## PRESENT VALUE OF $1
## USE WITH WORKSHEET IV

This value gives the present value of $1 received those years from today.

| | Annual Interest Rates: | | | | | | |
|---|---|---|---|---|---|---|---|
| Years | 4.00% | 5.00% | 6.00% | 7.00% | 8.00% | 9.00% | 10.00% |
| 1 | 0.9609 | 0.9514 | 0.9420 | 0.9326 | 0.9234 | 0.9143 | 0.9053 |
| 2 | 0.9233 | 0.9051 | 0.8872 | 0.8698 | 0.8526 | 0.8359 | 0.8195 |
| 3 | 0.8871 | 0.8610 | 0.8357 | 0.8111 | 0.7873 | 0.7642 | 0.7418 |
| 4 | 0.8524 | 0.8191 | 0.7871 | 0.7564 | 0.7270 | 0.6987 | 0.6715 |
| 5 | 0.8191 | 0.7793 | 0.7414 | 0.7055 | 0.6713 | 0.6387 | 0.6078 |
| 6 | 0.7870 | 0.7413 | 0.6984 | 0.6579 | 0.6198 | 0.5840 | 0.5502 |
| 7 | 0.7562 | 0.7053 | 0.6578 | 0.6135 | 0.5723 | 0.5339 | 0.4981 |
| 8 | 0.7266 | 0.6709 | 0.6196 | 0.5722 | 0.5285 | 0.4881 | 0.4509 |
| 9 | 0.6981 | 0.6383 | 0.5836 | 0.5336 | 0.4880 | 0.4463 | 0.4081 |
| 10 | 0.6708 | 0.6072 | 0.5497 | 0.4976 | 0.4506 | 0.4080 | 0.3695 |

Note: These values are rounded but should result in reasonably accurate answers.
These values ignore income taxes.
These values assume monthly compounding.
If you have a fractional interest rate (for example 6.25%), use the lower interest rate (6% for example) for determining the factor in this table.

# FINANCIAL TABLE II

## FUTURE VALUE OF $1
## USE WITH WORKSHEET V

This value gives the future value of $1 compounded monthly at the interest rate for those years.

| | Annual Interest Rates: | | | | | | |
|---|---|---|---|---|---|---|---|
| Years | 4.00% | 5.00% | 6.00% | 7.00% | 8.00% | 9.00% | 10.00% |
| 1 | 1.0407 | 1.0511 | 1.0616 | 1.0722 | 1.0829 | 1.0938 | 1.1047 |
| 2 | 1.0831 | 1.1049 | 1.1271 | 1.1498 | 1.1728 | 1.1964 | 1.2203 |
| 3 | 1.1272 | 1.1614 | 1.1966 | 1.2329 | 1.2702 | 1.3086 | 1.3481 |
| 4 | 1.1731 | 1.2208 | 1.2704 | 1.3220 | 1.3756 | 1.4314 | 1.4893 |
| 5 | 1.2209 | 1.2833 | 1.3488 | 1.4176 | 1.4898 | 1.5656 | 1.6453 |
| 6 | 1.2707 | 1.3490 | 1.4320 | 1.5201 | 1.6135 | 1.7125 | 1.8175 |
| 7 | 1.3225 | 1.4180 | 1.5203 | 1.6299 | 1.7474 | 1.8732 | 2.0079 |
| 8 | 1.3763 | 1.4905 | 1.6141 | 1.7478 | 1.8924 | 2.0489 | 2.2181 |
| 9 | 1.4324 | 1.5668 | 1.7136 | 1.8741 | 2.0495 | 2.2411 | 2.4504 |
| 10 | 1.4908 | 1.6470 | 1.8193 | 2.0096 | 2.2196 | 2.4513 | 2.7070 |

Note: These values are rounded but should result in reasonably accurate answers.
These values ignore income taxes.
These values assume monthly compounding.
If you have a fractional interest rate (for example 6.25%) use the lower interest rate (for example 6%) for determining the factor in this table.

# FINANCIAL TABLE III

## MONTHLY ANNUITY AMOUNT TO ACCUMULATE $1
## USE WITH WORKSHEET VI

This value results in the monthly deposit needed to accumulate $1 at the rate for those years.

| Years | Annual Interest Rates: 4.00% | 5.00% | 6.00% | 7.00% | 8.00% | 9.00% | 10.00% |
|---|---|---|---|---|---|---|---|
| 1 | 0.0819 | 0.0815 | 0.0811 | 0.0807 | 0.0804 | 0.0800 | 0.0796 |
| 2 | 0.0401 | 0.0398 | 0.0394 | 0.0390 | 0.0386 | 0.0382 | 0.0379 |
| 3 | 0.0262 | 0.0259 | 0.0255 | 0.0251 | 0.0247 | 0.0244 | 0.0240 |
| 4 | 0.0193 | 0.0189 | 0.0185 | 0.0182 | 0.0178 | 0.0174 | 0.0171 |
| 5 | 0.0151 | 0.0148 | 0.0144 | 0.0140 | 0.0137 | 0.0133 | 0.0130 |
| 6 | 0.0124 | 0.0120 | 0.0116 | 0.0113 | 0.0109 | 0.0106 | 0.0102 |
| 7 | 0.0104 | 0.0100 | 0.0097 | 0.0093 | 0.0090 | 0.0086 | 0.0083 |
| 8 | 0.0089 | 0.0085 | 0.0082 | 0.0079 | 0.0075 | 0.0072 | 0.0069 |
| 9 | 0.0078 | 0.0074 | 0.0071 | 0.0067 | 0.0064 | 0.0061 | 0.0058 |
| 10 | 0.0068 | 0.0065 | 0.0062 | 0.0058 | 0.0055 | 0.0052 | 0.0049 |

Note: These values are rounded but should result in reasonably accurate answers.
These values ignore income taxes.
These values assume monthly compounding.
If you have a fractional interest rate (for example 6.25%) use the lower interest rate (for example 6%) for determining the factor in this table.

# FINANCIAL TABLE IV

## FUTURE VALUE OF MONTHLY DEPOSITS
## USE WITH WORKSHEET VII

This value gives the future value if you deposit $1 every month at the rate for those years.

| | Annual Interest Rates: | | | | | | |
|---|---|---|---|---|---|---|---|
| Years | 4.00% | 5.00% | 6.00% | 7.00% | 8.00% | 9.00% | 10.00% |
| 1 | 12.2224 | 12.2788 | 12.3355 | 12.3925 | 12.4499 | 12.5075 | 12.5655 |
| 2 | 24.9428 | 25.1859 | 25.4319 | 25.6810 | 25.9331 | 26.1884 | 26.4469 |
| 3 | 38.1815 | 38.7533 | 39.3361 | 39.9301 | 40.5355 | 41.1527 | 41.7818 |
| 4 | 51.9596 | 53.0148 | 54.0978 | 55.2092 | 56.3499 | 57.5207 | 58.7224 |
| 5 | 66.2989 | 68.0060 | 69.7700 | 71.5929 | 73.4768 | 75.4241 | 77.4370 |
| 6 | 81.2225 | 83.7642 | 86.4088 | 89.1609 | 92.0253 | 95.0070 | 98.1113 |
| 7 | 96.7541 | 100.3286 | 104.0739 | 107.9989 | 112.1133 | 116.4269 | 120.9504 |
| 8 | 112.9185 | 117.7405 | 122.8285 | 128.1988 | 133.8685 | 139.8561 | 146.1810 |
| 9 | 129.7414 | 136.0431 | 142.7398 | 149.8589 | 157.4295 | 165.4832 | 174.0537 |
| 10 | 147.2498 | 155.2822 | 163.8793 | 173.0848 | 182.9460 | 193.5142 | 204.8449 |

Note: These values are rounded but should result in reasonably accurate answers.
These values ignore income taxes.
These values assume monthly compounding.
If you have a fractional interest rate (for example 6.25%) use the lower interest rate (for example 6%) for determining the factor in this table.

If you are interested in other books published by the Career Advancement Center, write to us and we will send you a catalog.

If the Personal Budget Planner is not available in your local bookstore, please order it directly from the publisher. Send a check or money order for $19.95 for each copy, plus $2.50 shipping and handling made out to "Career Advancement Center, Inc." (Post Office Box 436, Woodmere, New York 11598-0436). Please allow 4-6 weeks for delivery.